LITTLE,
BROWN

LB

**LARGE
PRINT**

Closer

YOUNG READERS EDITION

MARIANO RIVERA

with Wayne Coffey

Adapted for Young Readers by Sue Corbett

LITTLE, BROWN AND COMPANY

LARGE PRINT EDITION

Little, Brown and Company
Hachette Book Group
237 Park Avenue, New York, NY 10017

Visit us at lb-kids.com

Little, Brown and Company is a division of Hachette Book Group, Inc. The Little, Brown name and logo are trademarks of Hachette Book Group, Inc.

The publisher is not responsible for websites (or their content) that are not owned by the publisher.

First Edition: September 2014
First Large Print Edition: September 2014

Unless otherwise noted, all photographs are courtesy of the Rivera family.

Library of Congress Cataloging-in-Publication Data

Rivera, Mariano, 1969–
   The closer: young readers edition / Mariano Rivera with Wayne Coffey ; adapted for young readers by Sue Corbett.
      pages cm
   ISBN 978-0-316-40480-8 (hardback)—ISBN 978-0-316-28414-1 (ebook)—ISBN 978-0-316-28415-8 (library edition ebook)—ISBN 978-0-316-40962-9 (large print)   1. Rivera, Mariano, 1969–   2. Baseball players—Panama—Biography.   I. Title.
   GV865.R496R58 2014
   796.357092—dc23
   [B]

2014015176

10 9 8 7 6 5 4 3 2 1

RRD-C

Printed in the United States of America

To my Lord and Savior, Jesus Christ, and the family He has blessed me with: My beautiful wife, Clara, and our three wonderful boys, Mariano Jr., Jafet, and Jaziel

Contents

Prologue

It is a beautiful fall day in the Bronx, New York, nearly seventy degrees and sunny. We are hosting the San Francisco Giants, who have already been eliminated from the play-offs, while we are fighting for our postseason lives, three games behind the leader for the wild-card spot, with three teams ahead of us.

It is September 22, 2013.

It is also, unbelievably, "Mariano Rivera Day."

I have played nineteen years for the New York Yankees, but this season is my last. It is a bittersweet reality.

The Yankees have planned some sort of celebration of my career but have kept me in the dark about the details. My wife, Clara, and my three sons will be there, but that is all I know. I suit up early for the pregame festivities, and then I wait in one of the tunnels behind the outfield for my cue to enter the stadium.

One of the things I am known for is my calm demeanor. My cool exterior is not an act. I have never been prone to get nervous in a tight spot.

I am nervous right now.

On a piece of paper, I have written some inadequate words of thanks—to my parents, to my family, to my teammates, to the Yankee staff, most of all, to the fans. I slip the paper into my back pocket. I don't want words to fail me in this moment.

Finally, they tell me, "You're on, Mo."

There is a crowd in Monument Park, the

museum behind the center-field face where the Yankees display the retired numbers of their finest players, and the number 42, which was worn by Jackie Robinson, the first African American man to play Major League Baseball.

Because of his extraordinary contributions, baseball retired Robinson's number in 1997. But at the time, there were thirteen major league players still wearing 42, including me. We were allowed to keep the number until our careers ended.

I am the last active player still wearing No. 42. I have cherished being able to honor Mr. Robinson in this way.

Now, on Mariano Rivera Day, Mr. Robinson's 42, painted in the vivid blue of the team he played for—the Dodgers—has been replaced with a bronze plaque and given a prominent place of honor in Monument Park.

In the spot where his plaque had been hanging, at the end of a row of numbers the Yankees have already retired—Lou Gehrig's No. 4, Babe Ruth's No. 3, Joe DiMaggio's No. 5—there is a new No. 42, this one painted in Yankee blue against a pin-striped background.

This is *my* No. 42 that the Yankees are retiring on Mariano Rivera Day. Beneath it is a plaque that reads:

MARIANO RIVERA

"Mo" is considered the greatest closer in baseball history. He spent his entire career in pinstripes, from 1995–2013 and became the franchise leader in games pitched. Thriving under pressure, he amassed the most saves in postseason history. A 13-time All-Star, he retired as baseball's all-time saves leader.

I feel like my heart is going to come out of my chest. "Wow," I say out loud. I am so unbelievably humbled.

What am I doing here? I think to myself. How could this be happening to a skinny boy from a poor fishing village on the southern coast of Panama, a boy who didn't even have a glove when he tried out for the Yankees?

My amazement continues.

In the outfield, the heavy metal band Metallica is performing their song "Enter Sandman." It is the entrance music the Yankees play every time I come in to close a game. I pump my fist at the band. I am not a heavy metal music fan, but the band and I will be forever connected by this song.

I make the walk through the outfield to the mound, where there are more people who want to say goodbye, more tributes.

These formal goodbyes have been going on all season—The Mariano Rivera Farewell Tour. Some teams, like the Minnesota Twins, who I always pitched well against, are no doubt very happy to see me go. The Los Angeles Dodgers give me a fishing pole. The Texas Rangers give me a cowboy hat and boots. The Yankees have a special gift, too—it is a rocking chair.

Finally, they hand me a microphone. What can I say that will express to this crowd of

50,000 people what they, what my career, what being a New York Yankee, has meant to me? I completely forget about the note in my back pocket, but I remember to thank my family, my teammates, the fans, most of all. Words do start to fail me, so I say the two words dearest to the heart of any baseball player, or any baseball fan: "Play ball!"

Derek Jeter, who has been my teammate for two decades, since way back in Double-A ball in Greensboro, North Carolina, gives me a hug and a pat on the back. "You kept it together pretty good," he says. "I thought you were going to cry."

I didn't cry.

Not then.

The tears would come, eventually, but they would not be tears of sadness. They would be tears of joy from a fisherman's son whose dreams not only came true, but arrived bigger than he would ever have dared to imagine.

A Fisherman's Son

You don't mess around with machetes. I learn that as a little kid—decades before I ever hear of a cut fastball, much less throw one. I learn that you don't just pick one up and start swinging it as if it were a bat or a broomstick. You have to know how to use it, know the right technique, so you can be efficient and keep it simple, which, if you ask me, is the best way to go in all aspects of life.

Keep it simple.

My grandfather Manuel Giron teaches me everything I know about using a machete. We head out into the sugarcane fields and he shows me how to grip it—how to bend my knees and bring the blade around so it is level with the surface you want to cut, not a random whack but something much more precise. Once I get the hang of it, I cut our whole lawn with a machete. The lawn isn't big—closer to the size of a pitcher's mound than an outfield—but I still cut every square inch with that handheld blade. It takes an hour, maybe two. I never rush. It feels good when I am done.

I do not have my machete with me on the morning in late March 1990 when I walk out into the rising sun, breathing in the usual strong odor of fish arising from the shore by my home. I will not need the machete that day, nor the next.

I am twenty years old. I have just signed a contract to play baseball for the New York Yankees. I am not sure what this means, but I have hope: hope that my days of using a machete to cut the lawn, or working on my father's fishing boat, have ended, at least for a little while anyway.

A few weeks earlier, a Yankee scout named Herb Raybourn sits at the kitchen table in my family's home, a two-room cement house up the street from the beach in Puerto Caimito, the fishing village where I've lived my whole life. My parents sleep in one room; all four of us kids sleep in the other. We keep a couple of chickens out back. There is no wire strung over our house for a telephone—we don't have one—but there is a tree whose branches droop close to the tin roof when they get heavy with mangoes.

Before Herb arrives, I tell my father that a gringo is on his way to offer me a chance to play professional baseball. My father agrees to listen to what Señor Raybourn has to say. As it turns out, Herb is Panamanian and speaks Spanish, even though he looks white. He puts some papers on the kitchen table.

"The New York Yankees would like to sign

you to a contract and can offer you two thousand dollars," Herb says. "We think you are a young man with talent and a bright future."

Herb adds that the Yankees will include a glove and baseball cleats in the deal. At the time, I am making fifty dollars a week working on my father's fishing boat.

"Because you are twenty, we're not going to send you to the Dominican Republic, the way we do with teenagers," Herb continues. "We're going to send you right to Tampa for spring training."

The way he says it makes me think that going to Tampa (Where is Tampa? I wonder) rather than the Dominican Republic is good news, but I don't react because I don't want Sr. Raybourn to know just how clueless his newest signee is. I may have never heard of Tampa, but I know almost nothing about the Dominican Republic, either. My world isn't just small. It is the size of a marble. The farthest from home I have ever been is to the border of Costa Rica, a six-hour car ride west.

This is how little I understand about how professional baseball works: I think if I sign with the Yankees I will continue to play baseball in Panama. I figure I'll move to Panama City, get a better-looking uniform, along with a legit glove and a pair of shoes that don't have a hole in the big toe—like the ones I wore for my Yankee tryout. I'll get to play ball, make a little money, and then fulfill my real goal: to become a mechanic. I am pretty good at fixing things. I like fixing things. If I can make money playing baseball, maybe I can save enough to pay for mechanic's school.

What I know about the big leagues—*las Grandes Ligas*—is close to nothing. I know Rod Carew, Panama's greatest ballplayer, played there. I know there are two leagues, American and National, and that there is a World Series at the end of the season. That's it. I am already in the major leagues when I first hear somebody mention Hank Aaron.

"Who is Hank Aaron?" I ask.

"You're not serious," the guy says.

"Yes, I am. Who is Hank Aaron?"

"He's baseball's all-time home run leader, the guy who hit seven hundred fifty-five homers to beat Babe Ruth's record," the guy tells me.

"Who is Babe Ruth?" I ask.

The guy shakes his head in disbelief and turns away.

So Herb has to spell everything out for me, a kid as skinny as a Q-tip, and utterly naive: "No, you won't be staying in Panama," he says. "When you sign with a big league organization, you move to the United States." He advises me to spend a little of my bonus money on some shirts, underwear, and a suitcase to put them in. "You'll probably be a little nervous since you don't speak English."

This is a colossal understatement. I am not nervous. I am terrified. But I try not to let on. I don't want Herb to decide I'm not such a good prospect after all.

Weeks pass. The plane ticket to Tampa arrives. Now it is getting real.

Now it is time.

"*Vamos*, Pili," my mother says. Pili is the name my sister, Delia, gave me when I was a baby. Nobody knows why. It's what my family has called me my whole life.

My father starts our pickup truck, nicknamed "Turbo." It is ten years old, rusty and battered, and not anybody's idea of a race car, but to us? It's Turbo.

Clara Diaz Chacón, my sweetheart, sits in the front, between my father, Mariano Sr., and my mother, also named Delia. I throw my new suitcase in the flatbed and then climb in myself, along with my cousin Alberto. My father puts Turbo in reverse and we pull out of the driveway, onto Via Puerto Caimito, the one road in and out of our village, the only road that is paved.

We pass through Chorrera, a bigger town five miles east where, briefly, I went to high school, and then make our way on a twisty, rutted road, past goats and plantain trees and swatches of rain forest. Alberto and I bounce around in the back as if we are coconuts, anchored by nothing, only a skimpy railing to keep us from tumbling out.

I know where we are going—Tocumen International Airport in Panama City—but I am much less certain about where I am going.

I am a high school dropout. I don't even make it out of ninth grade at Pedro Pablo Sanchez High School, a U-shaped building with a courtyard where stray dogs sleep in whatever patch of shade they can find. It is a terrible decision to leave school, but I get fed up one day and bail, passing the sleeping dogs on my way out, in my pressed blue trousers and crisp white shirt. (I iron the uniform myself; I like things neat.) I am not thinking through the consequences of quitting school, and my parents don't talk me out of it. They are working-class people who are smart but not sold on the benefits of finishing school, earning a degree.

My last school lesson—and the last straw—comes in Señora Tejada's math class. She never tries to hide her dislike of me, glaring as if my presence in her classroom is a personal offense. I hang around with kids who aren't full-fledged troublemakers but are definitely into mischief. It is guilt by association, I guess.

One day, a few of us are fooling around, paying little attention to the Pythagorean theorem and lots of attention to the kid we are tormenting. One of my friends crumples up a piece of paper and hits the kid in the head with it.

"Hey, cut it out," the kid says.

I am not the pitcher in this case, but I do laugh.

"Rivera!" Señora Tejada always calls me by my last name. "Why did you throw that?"

"I didn't throw anything," I say.

"Don't tell me you didn't throw it. Come up here," she demands.

I didn't do anything wrong. I am not going anywhere.

"Rivera, come up here!" she repeats.

Again, I defy a direct order, and now she is really ticked off. She walks over to my desk and stands over me.

"You are to leave this classroom right now," she says, escorting me into the hallway, where I spend the rest of math class not doing math.

The principal suspends me for three days, but it turns out to be a much longer sentence than that. I never return to Pedro Pablo Sanchez High School. I don't see Señora Tejada again, either, until I run into her in a market after I've been in pro ball for several years.

"*¡Hola, Mariano!*" she says. (Notice we are on a first-name basis now.) "Congratulations on your baseball career. I've followed how well you are doing."

No glare. No scolding voice. She greets me like a favorite student she hasn't seen since graduation.

The best I can do is force a weak smile. People should not treat you according to how successful or prominent you are. The whole time I was in her class, she regarded me as a juvenile delinquent. Maybe I wasn't going to be the next Albert Einstein, but I was nowhere near the bad kid she made me out to be.

Please don't pretend that you like me now when you didn't care about me at all when I was a student, I think.

"Thanks," I tell her curtly, heading right past her to the fruit aisle.

But Señora Tejada isn't the only reason I drop out of school. Another big problem is fighting, a regular occurrence. In the hallways, in the schoolyard, on the way back home—fights break out everywhere, almost always for the same reason: kids teasing me about the way I smell.

There he goes, the fishy boy.

Hold your nose, the fish are getting closer.

I thought we were in school, not on the fishing boat.

My tormentors are right. I do smell like fish. Plenty of Puerto Caimito kids do. We live by the water, not far from a processing plant that makes fish meal out of sardines— *harina de pescado*, as we call it. My father is a captain on a commercial fishing boat, his long workdays spent throwing his nets and hauling in all the sardines and anchovies he can. The smell of fish overpowers everything in Puerto Caimito. You could shower for an hour and plunge yourself in cologne, and if a droplet or two of water from the fish plant touches your clothes, you will stink all night. But fish keep the local economy afloat. Fish supply jobs for the parents of the kids who are taunting me. I could, should ignore them. I do not.

They bait me, and then they reel me in. I'm not proud of this. It's really dumb on my part. I should turn the other cheek, as the Bible teaches. But I am young and headstrong, intent on doing things my own way.

We continue the drive to the airport. We are on the *autopista*, the main highway. The warm air rushes across my face in the back of the pickup. I am getting sadder. We drive past groves of mango and pineapple trees and fields full of cows, and it's almost as if my childhood is passing by, too. I think about playing ball on the beach with a glove made from a milk carton, a bat made from a stick, and a ball made from tightly wound fishing nets. I wonder if I've played my last game on El Tamarindo, a dirt patch of a field named for the tamarind tree by home plate. I think about what would've happened if I'd kept playing soccer, my first sporting love, trying to beat defenders with a ball attached to my foot (with or without shoes), imagining myself the Panamanian Pelé, a dream that lasted until I got smacked in the eye with the ball during a game and temporarily lost vision. I kept playing and, twenty minutes later, went up for a header, collided with a guy, and wound up in the emergency room, where the doctor closed the cut and told me the eye looked very bad and needed to be seen by a specialist.

My soccer career ended after that.

We are just a half hour away now. I look into Turbo's cab, at Clara, sitting between my parents. We live just a few houses apart in Puerto Caimito; I've known her since kindergarten. She stops speaking to me when I drop out of school, so disappointed that I'd just quit like that. She expects more from me. The deep freeze lasts until a bunch of us are at a club one night, and Clara and I wind up dancing. Friendship turns to romance, and as the music ends, our eyes lock and she reaches for my wrist. I know I am forgiven, and I know the reason she was mad at me was because she was serious about our relationship.

After I leave school, I hang around the clubs in Chorrera a lot, whenever I am not out at sea on my father's boat. I love to dance—Merengue Mariano, they call me. The merengue is a popular dance in the Caribbean and Central America. I am not closing any baseball games, only closing nightclubs.

As with a lot of clubs, the cops are regular

visitors because fights are commonplace. Guys pack ice picks or knives. One night I am there with a big group, fifteen kids, maybe more. One friend gets into an argument with a kid who is with a big group of his own. I don't know how it starts, probably a look or a comment about somebody's girl, the usual stuff. It's getting heated. They are about to go at it when I step between them.

"Guys, we're here to have fun and dance, not fight," I say. "Let's not do anything foolish."

They posture and act tough and curse at each other, but they back off. Then someone in the other group pushes his way to the front. He is carrying a machete. The look on his face suggests he wants to use it, and not on a patch of grass. Apparently he wants the fight to go on, specifically with me.

"Where's that skinny kid, the peacemaker?" he yells, brandishing the long blade.

I am back in the crowd by now, but I hear him. I have no weapon, but I have common sense, and a lot of speed. I take off running. The guy chases me, but I leave him in the dust. He never finds me.

Getting chased by the kid with the machete is another wake-up call. When Clara and I start seeing each other regularly, we go out for quiet dinners, or lie in the hammock that is strung between two trees next to my parents' house. We talk all the time and I finally realize:

Nothing good is going to happen to me if I keep dancing the night away in the clubs.

It is Clara who makes me understand I want more out of life than to be a fisherman by day and Merengue Mariano by night.

My father wheels Turbo into the airport and parks. Alberto and I climb out of the back. We all walk toward the terminal. What's about to happen is hitting me hard.

I am leaving home. Leaving Panama.

Leaving Clara.

I am a professional baseball player from this moment on, all six feet, one hundred and fifty pounds of me. I don't know how long it will last. There is no hiding my feelings now; I am scared. I know I love to play ball, but have no idea how I will measure up to other players. I am not a worrier by nature, but I am a realist. Has anybody else made this transition, from Panamanian fishing boat to the New York Yankees?

"I came to Puerto Caimito to be a fisherman," my father says. "I started at the bottom, cleaning boats, sweeping up garbage, getting paid pennies, but I worked hard and I advanced and finally became a captain. You will do the same, Pili. It won't be easy, but you are going to work your way to the top."

I hug my mother goodbye and shake my father's hand.

I am not going to see Clara for five months. It feels as if it will be five years.

I tell Clara how much I will miss her. I will write and I will be back soon, I say. I try not to cry, but I do anyway.

She is crying, too. "I love you, Pili. I will be here, waiting for your safe return," she says.

I make my way through the ticket counter and wait to pass through security. I hear my mother say, "There goes our boy. I wonder where this is going to take him?" I do not turn around. If I see their faces, I may change my mind.

They head upstairs toward a viewing deck to watch the plane take off. I turn and walk down a passageway, onto the plane. Soon I am airborne, the first flight of my life. My tears are almost dry. I do not look back.

NOTES FROM MO

Béisbol School

Baseball has been called America's "National Pastime," but *Latin* American players have become a very important part of the game. At the start of the 2013 season, nearly one-quarter of the players on Major League Baseball rosters hailed from Latin America, including some of the game's biggest stars: Miguel Cabrera, David Ortiz, Jose Reyes, Albert Pujols, and Robinson Canó.

Latino players come from places like Venezuela, Mexico, Puerto Rico, Cuba, and Panama, but no matter where a *buscone* (that's the Spanish word for "scout") finds them, the first stop for virtually all Latino prospects is the Dominican Republic, where each MLB team runs its own baseball academy, with dormitories, playing fields, training facilities, clubhouses, and classrooms. It's no surprise that the foreign country with the highest number of players on MLB rosters is the DR, a poor country that occupies half the Caribbean island of Hispaniola. One small DR town, San Pedro de Macorís, is called the "cradle of shortstops" because so many of MLB's premier infielders have been born there, including Canó, Alfonso Soriano, Luis Castillo, and Juan Samuel.

While the primary focus at the academies is refining baseball talent, there are also educational programs, including language instruction, to help Spanish-speaking teenagers prepare for success either in the U.S. or after their playing careers have ended.

So why would Herb Raybourn make it sound like I lucked out by missing a stop in the DR?

Well, unlike with American kids, MLB regulations allow teams to sign Latino players before they finish high school, even as young as sixteen, when their bodies and their skills are far less developed. In the past, that has allowed many teams to acquire big-time talent at bargain-basement prices. Few American prospects sign for as little as a $20,000 bonus; the *buscones* have been known to sign *four* Latino sixteen-year-olds for that price. (I was thrilled with $2,000 in 1990.)

As a result, the competition to "graduate" from these academies is fierce: fewer than half the DR prospects will ever leave the island to play in the U.S. minor leagues. So, because I was twenty and considered "too old" for the Yankees' academy, I skipped a step where the careers of many prospects both begin—and end.

A Childhood on the Beach

From the air, you can see how small and vulnerable my country is. It's just a curvy strip of earth at the southern tip of Central America, not much wider than a shoelace.

Puerto Caimito, where I grew up, is about twenty-five miles west of our famous canal, on the Pacific side of Panama. It is a village put on the map by fish. If you aren't an actual fisherman in Puerto Caimito, then you probably repair boats, or work at the fish processing plant, or haul fish to market. Just about everybody is connected to fish, and everybody eats it.

"I ate fish every day, and that's what made me strong," my father says. My grandfather lived to be ninety-six, and my father predicts he will outlive that age. I wouldn't bet against him. He is from tough farmer stock. One of fifteen children, he was born in Darién, near the Colombian border. After he left school he spent eleven hours a day, six days a week, working on the family farm. They grew rice, corn, and plantains, and did it without a tractor or any other sort of power equipment. Shovels, hoes, rakes—that was high-end gear for well-to-do farmers. My father used a machete to cut brush and weeds, and sharp sticks to till the soil. Each week they would take their goods to the market, an all-day trip in a boat powered by a pole in the water, gondola-style.

It was a hard life, and by the time my father

was a teenager, several of his brothers had already moved to Puerto Caimito, because fishing was considered a more prosperous line of work. At age seventeen, my father joined them. He started out with whatever odd jobs he could get. He was still learning his way around when he went for a walk one day and saw a girl washing dishes and singing in front of her home. The girl, one of eight children herself, was fifteen years old. My father says it was love at first sight. Her name was Delia Girón, and two years after she stole my father's heart with her singing, she gave birth to a baby girl.

Two years after that, she gave birth to me, on November 29, 1969.

Growing up in Puerto Caimito is simple and smelly. For my first seventeen years we lived on the shore of the Gulf of Panama, in a dingy two-room house on a dirt road, just a long toss from the fish-meal plant. There's a whole neighborhood of such homes in the village, most of them occupied by my aunts and uncles and cousins. When my parents moved in, they had no electricity or running water. There was an outhouse in the backyard and a well for water a short walk away. When the sun sank into the Gulf, they lit the rooms with kerosene lamps. By the time I came around in 1969, the house had gotten several upgrades: electricity and water, but still no bathroom.

The beach is just steps away but it is strewn with broken shells, pieces of old boats, and fragments of discarded net. It is not the beach in a tourist advertisement—no turquoise water or tropical trees or sand as soft as baby powder. It's a working place, a storm-battered boat here, half a dead fish there, the litter of people who make a living from the sea.

But this shore is where I became an athlete. At low tide it offers the best playing field in Puerto Caimito, wide and long. You could run forever on the mudflats. I play soccer here.

I play baseball here. My favorite game is the one where we get a piece of cardboard, cut out three holes in it, and string it up between two sticks in the sand. Then we stand back about twenty or thirty feet and fire rocks and see who can get the most rocks through the holes.

My aim is good.

We have no bat, so we find an old piece of wood or saw off the branch of a tree. We have no ball, so we wrap up a rock with fishnet and tape. We have no baseball gloves, but you can make one out of cardboard, if you know how to fold it.

This is how I play ball for almost all of my childhood; I don't put a real glove on my hand until I am sixteen years old. My father buys it for me, secondhand, right before we move away from the shore, up the street about a third of a mile, to another cement-block house in a quieter location.

Neither of our homes ever had a telephone. I don't have my own bicycle. I have only one toy. It's called Mr. Big Mouth. You touch his belly and his big mouth opens and you put a little chip in it. I don't feel deprived, because I am not deprived. It's just the way life is.

I have everything I need.

My favorite time of year is Christmas. As the oldest boy in the family, my job is to get our Christmas tree. I do it every year, and know just where to go. Behind our house is a *manglar*—a swamp—that has a lot of little trees growing in the muck. You aren't going to find a tall evergreen tree in the swamp, of course, so the next best thing is something three or four feet tall that I can yank out with a strong tug. I bring it home, and after it dries out, we wrap the branches in cloth so it looks festive. Santa Claus never makes it to our part of Panama—there are certainly no chimneys—but *Noche Buena*, our name for Christmas Eve, is still magical, with lights twinkling and Christmas songs playing and all the anticipation of the big day.

I discover early on that I love to run, and I love to be in motion. If I am not playing soccer or baseball, I am playing basketball. When the tide is in and the beach shrinks, we move to El Tamarindo, just far enough off the shore to let us play without being ankle-deep in mud. Whatever I play, I want to win badly. When a baseball victory is about to turn into a defeat, I throw the ball into the Gulf of Panama and declare the game a tie. It doesn't win me any sportsmanship awards, but it prevents a loss.

I also like to hunt iguanas. They are everywhere in Panama, green and spiky and leathery, six-foot-long lizards that lounge on branches and hide in the vegetation. I know exactly where to find them, and how to hunt them. All I need is a rock. Iguanas are very fast, and they are amazingly resilient; they can fall forty or fifty feet out of a tree and run away as if they'd just slid off a park bench. But most of the time, iguanas are stationary, resting on the upper branches of trees, and that makes them an easy target. Most times I'd have a direct hit on the first try, pick it up, and sling it over my shoulder to bring home for dinner. "Chicken of the trees," we call it. It's not a staple like coconut rice or tamales, and you aren't going to find fast-food restaurants selling iguana nuggets, but it's one of my favorite dishes.

I never stop to figure out how many relatives I have in Puerto Caimito, but my cousins might outnumber the iguanas. There are always enough around for a game. But when you grow up with a big family in a small town, it's almost impossible to do anything without everybody knowing about it.

This is not always a good thing when you have a father like mine.

My father is a great provider who rises before dawn on Monday and spends all week on his fishing boat, twelve to fourteen hours a day hauling and dragging the nets. I don't remember him ever taking a day off. Vacation? Sick days?

No such thing. He is a fisherman. Fishermen fish.

But he is a stern disciplinarian. As a kid, mostly what I associate with my father is fear. He is a big, strong man. I am a small, skinny kid. He has not heard that spanking your child, or taking your belt to his backside, is out of fashion with other parents. When I know I've messed up and that the belt is coming, I put on two pairs of pants. Sometimes I put on three pairs of pants. You need all the cushioning you get.

My father's brother—my uncle Miguel—lives next door to us. He is very tough on his kids, too. He works on the boat with my father. I am very close to him, so one time I decide to ask my uncle straight-out.

"Why are you and my father so rough on your children? Do you want us to live in fear of you?"

My uncle thinks about it for a few moments. "If you think we are tough, you should've seen how our father was with us," he says. "This is not an excuse, but this is all we know, because it is how we were raised. We left home as soon as we could—to get away from it."

I think about my father as a kid, being afraid of his own father, leaving home when he wasn't much more than a boy. It is hard to imagine. But repeating that hurtful pattern with us is not the solution. That is something I learn from him as well.

NOTES FROM MO

My Country

Panama is not a big country, nor a rich country. There are 3.6 million residents, way less than half the population of New York City.

If not for the canal, many people would have never heard of the place where I was born. But the Panama Canal is a key passage for trade and transportation, and it has made Panama important to the rest of the world.

The canal was started by France in 1864 and finished by the United States in 1914. It cuts through the entire width of the country. Panama is narrow and the canal is only about fifty miles long. Nonetheless, this engineering marvel provides a way for ships to travel from the Atlantic Ocean to the

Pacific without having to go around South America, a shortcut that saves time, enormous amounts of fuel, and about eight thousand miles of sea travel.

Panama isn't just a place where two oceans meet; it's also place where two continents, North and South America, are linked. On the west, the country borders Costa Rica, in Central America. On the east, Panama borders Colombia, in South America.

For a nation that is a little smaller than the state of South Carolina, it has a lot of strategic importance.

My First Job

By the time I am eighteen years old, I am working full-time on my father's boat, the youngest of nine crew members. The *Lisa*, as the boat is named, is a hulking steel vessel with a banged-up hull and a rusty patchwork of dents and dark paint. It has seen better days.

I am not on board because I want to be. I am on board to make my fifty dollars a week so I can go to mechanic's school. I have already decided that the fisherman's life is not for me. I don't like being out at sea, the long hours, the monotony. I don't like the risks.

"Did you know that fishing is the second-most-dangerous occupation, behind logging?" a friend asks me. "That it's thirty-six times more dangerous than the average job?"

"I didn't know that," I reply. But I am not surprised. A family friend had his arm ripped right off his body when it got caught between two boats.

There is another reason I am not keen on being a fisherman. I hate being away from Clara. Six days a week at sea, and one day a week with Clara? I would like to reverse this ratio.

Right now I don't have a choice, though. I need money and this is how I can earn it. We are in the Gulf of Panama with our nets in the water. For hours we've been in one of our regular sardine hot spots, called *La Maestra*, but we haven't caught anything. So, we head back to our base island. We are about twenty minutes away, not far from the Canal, when the fish-finding sonar lights up.

You are not supposed to fish near the Panama Canal. There is too much traffic on the seas, and the other boats don't slow down. With a boat the size of my father's—ninety feet in length and 120 tons in weight, with nets that stretch out a thousand feet—it's not easy to get out of the way if you have to.

But my father has a motto I have heard my whole life:

The nets don't make money on the boat. They only make money in the water.

If the sonar is orange, it means you've come across a lot of fish. If the sonar is red, it means you have hit the fish lottery. The sonar is red. They are everywhere. We go all day with no action, and suddenly we're right on top of the mother of all sardine schools. Even though we're near the Canal, my father figures that at this late hour, boat traffic won't be a problem.

"Drop the net!" my father hollers.

We cast the net out in a huge circle, the

idea being to surround the fish with it, and then quickly cinch it closed with two massive ropes that are pulled tight like a drawstring by hydraulic winches.

We have a huge haul, maybe eighty or ninety tons of sardines, the net just about bursting. We have so many fish, in fact, that my father radios other boats to meet us so we can transfer our haul, then return to catch more.

It is now close to 4:00 a.m. It's not normal to fish at this hour, but we don't stop when the sonar is red.

My father circles the spot again and we drop the net. He has a hard time maneuvering the boat in the strong current. There is one guy in the back and one in the front working the ropes—huge hunks of braided line that do the heavy lifting, bringing the bounty up to the boat. The ropes are guided by a pulley system, and at the top of the pulleys there are flaps that lock into place so the ropes won't fly out of control once the winch starts reeling them in. When the ropes retract, they move at a blinding clip, like cars on the Daytona straightaway.

We work in complete darkness, sunrise still two hours away. Our deck lights are off because lights would scare the fish away. We are about to close the net, fire up the hydraulic winches, and bring in our haul. I am near the middle of the boat, about six feet from my uncle Miguel. It's tricky to work without light, but we're all so familiar with what needs to be done that it isn't usually a problem.

Except that one of the pulley flaps is not secure. In the daytime, somebody definitely would've noticed. In the darkness, nobody does.

The ropes have to close the net in tandem, one after another, and when I notice that one rope is too far ahead, I tell the crew member on the second rope to let go of his rope. He lets go, but because the flap is not secure, when the winch starts reeling it in, the rope takes off, coming at us like a braided bazooka, ripping out of the water and onto the deck.

There is no time to get out of the way. The rope blasts into my uncle at chest level, knocking a 240-pound man across the ship as if he were a palm frond. He crashes face-first into the metal edge of a bin. The rope lashes into me a microsecond later, and I fly even farther, but I don't hit anything sharp.

I lose a tooth and get scraped and bruised but otherwise come out unscathed. It has nothing to do with athletic ability. I was lucky to be knocked sideways into a relatively safe place.

My uncle is not so fortunate. He is badly hurt. He is screaming in pain. It is the most horrific thing I've ever seen.

Everybody on board is screaming. My father, who is at the helm in the cabin upstairs, races down to find his brother looking as if he'd taken a machete to the face. I keep replaying the nightmarish sequence of events. An unfastened flap, an out-of-control rope, and seconds later, an uncle I love—the man who gently explained to me why my

father is so strict and quick with the belt—
seems about to die before my eyes.

My father radios the Coast Guard, and
they arrive within minutes to take my uncle
to the nearest hospital. The sun is coming up
now. I can't get the brutal images out of my
head.

My uncle fights for his life for a month.
He does not win. The funeral and burial are
held in Puerto Caimito. Hundreds of people
attend. "Miguel has gone home to be with
the Lord," the priest says. It is the first time I
remember seeing my father cry.

We are back out on the boat a few days
later, because the nets only make money in
the water. The perils of the job are nothing we
can change. This is what we do, day after day,
week after week.

Close to a year after my uncle's death, we are
churning toward Contadora Island, in the

Pacific Ocean near Colombia. The nets fill quickly and we return to unload our haul. We have not gotten far when the belt on our water pump stops working. We try the spare belt we keep on board, but it doesn't fit properly.

This is not good.

The pump is what gets the water out of the boat. You don't stay afloat for long with a dead pump.

We're carrying about a hundred tons of sardines, so we're sitting low, taking on water. Without the pump, we immediately begin taking on a lot more water. We are about two thousand feet from Pacheca, an island near Contadora, when we start to sink.

There is no time to deliberate. My father has an immediate decision to make.

"We're going to bring the boat into Pacheca, right onto the sand," my father says. There isn't time to get anywhere else.

He heads directly for the island and we are about halfway there, maybe a thousand feet away, when the belt mysteriously starts working again. Nobody knows why, and nobody is launching an investigation. Water begins to get pumped out and the boat rises. My father's relief is written on his face; he knows how risky it is to pilot such a big boat onto shore. We could hit a rock or a coral reef, and the hull would get shredded like cheese in a grater. We'd take on too much sandy water, gumming up and destroying the engine.

With the pump back in commission, my father says we're going back to Taboguilla, to unload the fish. The wind is picking up and the swells in the ocean are getting bigger, but my father has fished these waters for years, and has keen instincts about safety. Those instincts have served him well so far. He reverses and pulls away from Pacheca.

We don't get more than fifteen hundred feet before the pump stops again.

It is almost 9:00 p.m. The water in the boat starts rising again, but now the wind is stronger, and soon the swells are eight or ten feet, crashing over the sides of the boat. The conditions are worsening by the second. The boat is taking on water at a terrifying rate.

Now there is no decision to make, because there is only one option.

"We're heading back to Pacheca!" my father shouts. He turns the boat around. The shoreline is our only port in the storm.

It is not going to be an easy or fast trip, not with the water on board and the seas so rough.

Let's just get to safety, get to shore, no matter how slow going it is. I know this is what my father must be thinking.

And then the engine quits.

It doesn't sputter or wheeze. It just dies. The engine is in the front of the boat; it was probably swamped by all the water.

"Now what do we do?" I ask.

"Get down there and try to crank-start it," he says. He seems remarkably calm, given the circumstances.

We scurry down the metal steps into the hull, through the wet and darkness. I grip a thick metal handle and start turning a device that pumps air to generate power to jump-start the engine.

Nothing.

I crank some more. No response.

Our ninety-foot boat is sinking fast. We don't have time to keep trying. We scramble up to the main deck, where the water is almost waist-high.

"Everybody onto the lifeboat!" my father hollers.

The lifeboat is made of iron, deep-hulled and fifteen feet long. We fight the wind and walls of water and finally wrestle the lifeboat into the sea. All nine of us get in. It is supposed to be equipped with life jackets, but it isn't. My father starts the engine and steers us slowly away from the *Lisa*, waves crashing and cresting, tossing the lifeboat as if it were a bathtub toy.

Behind us, I see my father's boat—and our family's livelihood—keel onto its side and turn upside down. Within minutes, it disappears completely.

Pacheca is maybe eight hundred feet away, but it might as well be on the other side of the earth. The lifeboat is sitting so low with all of us in it that now it starts to take on water, too.

I look out toward the lights of Pacheca. Will I have to swim for my life? How many of us will make it? The swells are one thing. The sharks are another. We have fished these waters many times. Hammerheads, reef sharks, tiger sharks: There are sharks everywhere. Our best hope to reach shore is via the back side of the island, where there is some protection from the wind and the seas should be calmer. That is where my father tries to take us, but it is slow going. Up and down the swells we go. The big boat is already gone. Is this one going down, too?

I can't stop staring at the churning sea. It looks so angry. We inch closer to the island, but it still seems hopelessly far away. The wind and water continue to pound us. Nobody on the boat says a word. I can barely breathe.

I can't believe I might die because of a faulty water pump.

I knew I wanted no part of being a fisherman, and this is exactly why. I think about my uncle, and what the fishing life has cost our family. I think about my mother and brothers and sister. Most of all, I think about Clara. She is my best friend, the person I want to spend my life with, even though I haven't yet told her that. The thought that I might never see her again is too much to bear.

A wave of water soaks me as I hang on to the side of the boat. Do I want to drown to death, or get eaten by a shark? Nineteen years of age, and these are my options.

Somehow my father keeps the lifeboat creeping forward, plowing and dipping through the waves. Somehow, he makes progress. Maybe he will get us to the calmer water. Maybe we aren't going down.

Is it five minutes later? Ten minutes? I don't know. I just know we are closer, maybe three hundred feet from land. The wind is subsiding and the surf smoothes out. We pick up a little speed. We are heading toward a sandy beach.

We are going to make it to Pacheca.

My father guides the lifeboat onto the beach. I jump out and shout with joy.

"Land! We're on land. Land has never felt so good!"

We begin hugging each other. I even hug my father—that's a first, as far as I can remember—and thank him for doing such a masterful job. My father had radioed ahead, so the police and Coast Guard are waiting. They take us to a hotel, where our shivering and grateful group gets hot showers and dry clothes.

Eventually, my father gets a new boat, but for the time being, our fishing season is over. We spend our time repairing nets. I am happy to be doing anything, because it means I am alive.

The near calamity brings one other positive result: Without our six-day workweek on the boat, I have more time to play ball with my team, Panama Oeste. I played ball all the time as a kid, but in a place as poor and remote as Puerto Caimito, it's more likely to be a pickup game than anything remotely organized. I am one of the stronger players from our village, and at thirteen I am invited to join Panama Oeste, the team that represents the region in which I live, and travel around the country to play teams from other provinces. I am a good local player, but it's not as if people are touting me as the next Rod Carew. When I turn eighteen, I move up to the Panama Oeste Vaqueros, the Cowboys, in Panama's top adult league. I play wherever the Vaqueros want me to play. One game I am in right field, the next game at shortstop, and the one after that I am behind the plate. I usually bat leadoff or No. 2. I can hit the ball in the gaps, and I can run.

My favorite position, though, is the outfield, because there's nothing better in baseball than running down a fly ball. I am stationed in right field for an important game in the league playoffs. We have our best starter on the mound, but today our opponents are all over him, smacking hits from here to the Canal. We dig ourselves a big hole. The manager comes out to the mound, looks around for a moment, and then motions to me in right field.

Why is he looking at me? I think. *He can't mean me. I am not a pitcher.*

He points at me again. He waves for me to come in. He does mean me. I have no clue what is going on, but I trot in.

"I know you aren't a pitcher," the manager says, "but we're in a bind, and all we're looking for is for you to throw strikes. Don't worry about anything else. Throw the ball over the plate and you'll be fine."

"Well, I'll try, but I really don't know what I'm doing," I say.

"Throw strikes and you'll be fine," he says again.

"Okay, I'll do my best," I say.

I've always had a good arm, a loose arm, and I can pretty much put the ball where I want. But I am far from the hardest thrower around, and I haven't pitched since I threw a few innings for the provincial team when I was fourteen. It feels totally bizarre to have my foot on the rubber, to try to come up with some motion on the spot.

I come on in the second inning and go the rest of the way. I do not allow a run. I do nothing cute. I have no curveball and sure don't have any dipsy-do windup. I get the ball and throw it, probably no more than eighty-five miles per hour, but I am getting ahead of everybody, hitting corners, pitching quickly.

We win the game.

"Great job," the manager says. "You kept us in it and gave us time to come back. You saved the game for us."

I do not think any more about it. As far as I'm concerned, this is a one-day fling. Next time out, I will be at short or in right field again.

I go back to fixing the nets and playing as much ball with Oeste as I can while I have this unexpected break from fishing. I wonder if now is the time to enroll in mechanic's school. I am still thinking about that two weeks later when Clara and I are walking back from the beach on a Sunday afternoon. Outside the house, my teammates from Panama Oeste, Emilio Gaes and Claudino Hernández, are waiting for me. They want to speak to me, and, since we still have no phone, their showing up is the only way that will happen.

"What are you guys doing here?" I say.

"We've arranged a tryout for you," Claudino says.

"A tryout? What are you talking about? With who?"

"With the New York Yankees."

"The New York Yankees?" *Do you really expect me to believe this?* I think.

"Yes, they want to see you pitch," Claudino says.

"We told them how good you looked the other day and they think you are worth checking out," Emilio says.

This is getting more absurd by the second.

"See me pitch? But I am not a pitcher," I say. "If you guys are joking, please stop it."

"We are not joking. We're serious, Mariano. They want to see you pitch and the tryout is tomorrow," Claudino says.

I look at my teammates in complete disbelief. When I press for more details, Claudino tells me he was so impressed with the game I pitched in long relief that he called Chico Heron to tell him about me. Chico is a local coach and part-time scout for the Yankees, one of those baseball lifers who are always at one field or another. Emilio and Claudino are really good guys, but it turns out that if the Yankees sign a player you recommended to them, they pay a finder's fee of two hundred dollars.

"So what do you think?" Claudino asks.

What I think is that it's one of the craziest things I've ever heard. But nets don't make any money when they are on the boat. And I love playing ball.

"I'll see you tomorrow," I say.

Two Buses, Nine Pitches

The Yankees hold their tryout in Estadio Juan Demóstenes Arosemena, an ornate old park named for the Panamanian president who had it built in 1938. The Latin words *Citius, Altius, Fortius*—Faster, Higher, Stronger—are etched into the stone by the main entrance. I am not confident I will be any of the three, but I will give it my best shot.

I spend the first half of the day repairing nets with my father, who grudgingly gives me permission to take the afternoon off, as long as I get something done before I leave.

After lunch, I take a bus from Puerto Caimito to Chorrera. It costs forty-five cents. In Chorrera, I catch the bus to Panama City—an hour and a half away, but a public transportation bargain at sixty-five cents. By the time I arrive, I am hungry, so I stop at a bodega and get six little rolls—*pan de huevo*—for a nickel apiece, and a twenty-five-cent container of milk. I won't have the full $1.10 I need for the bus trip home, but the drivers are usually good about letting you slide until the next time.

It's a twenty-minute walk from the bus stop to the stadium. Much of it is through a barrio called Curundú, a ragged section of the city with run-down houses and starving dogs almost everywhere you look. You see drunks, homeless people, and street hustlers. Crime is widespread. It's not a neighborhood you want to linger in, but people tell me that nobody messes with ballplayers. I walk fast.

If the Yankees had a dress code for tryouts, I would've been sent right back to Puerto Caimito. I show up in old green pants, a frayed shirt, the shoe with the hole...and no glove. There are about twenty other prospects there, and when I arrive in my ragamuffin outfit, they point at me and laugh.

Hey, look, they're giving a tryout to a hobo, I imagine them saying.

I've played games in the park before. I know the layout and the size—it seats twenty-five thousand people—so the surroundings are familiar. The first thing I do is find Chico Heron, the scout. Chico is a small, round man who always has a Yankee hat on his curly mop of hair. I've known him for years; you can't be a ballplayer around Chorrera or Puerto Caimito and not know him. I say hello.

"I'm glad you're here, Mariano," he says. "I hear you looked good in relief the other day. So you are doing some pitching now?"

"Well, a little bit," I tell him, which is not

a complete lie. "It's not like I pitch every day or anything." Really, I just pitched that one time, because the team needed me.

"Okay, fine," he says. "Get out there and warm up and we'll get started."

Chico had scouted me once before, about a year earlier. He was looking at me as a shortstop when I played some games for Oeste. I made most of the plays, and had a couple of hits, but Chico didn't see enough to recommend me as a prospect. He was concerned that I wouldn't be a good enough hitter to make it in *las Grandes Ligas*, and because he'd scouted me previously, he wasn't all that fired up when he got the call from Claudino and Emilio.

"I've already seen Mariano Rivera as a shortstop," Chico told them.

"You haven't seen him as a pitcher," Emilio says.

"Trust me. I caught him," Claudino says, piling on. "This is a kid who can put the ball wherever he wants."

I recognize quite a few of the guys at the tryout from playing against them. At twenty years old, I am probably the oldest player there. The guy they really want to look at is a kid named Luis Parra, a really hard thrower. I ask one of the guys if I can borrow a glove to warm up. I am not worried about Luis Parra or anybody else. I'm not there to make an impression. I just want to play ball. *What's the worst they can do—send me home?* I am not thinking that this is my big chance to escape Puerto Caimito and change the course of my family's life forever.

After a few minutes, Chico calls me over.

"Why don't you get on the mound and throw some pitches?" he suggests.

I nod and head to the mound, digging in front of the rubber a little. When I look down I see my big toe poking out of my right shoe. I face the plate, pitch from the traditional windup position. I rock back with my left leg, raise my hands up slightly, then bring my left leg forward and push off with my right.

I wind and deliver—a fastball on the corner. I get the ball back and throw again, another strike on the black that pops into the catcher's glove. I am throwing easily, fluidly, with no grunting or flailing limbs. I may be built like a pipe cleaner, but I can put the ball where it needs to go.

I throw a total of nine pitches. They are all fastballs, because that is the only pitch I have.

"That's good, Mariano. That's all I need," Chico says.

I am not sure what he means. Nine pitches? That's it? Time to get back to the fishnets now?

A few minutes later, Chico pulls me aside.

"I like what I saw from you today," he says. "I would like you to keep coming back for the rest of the week, and then have Herb Raybourn, director of Latin American scouting for the Yankees, take a look at you. Herb is the one who makes the final call. What do you think about that?"

"As long as I can get off of work, I'll come

back," I tell him. "Thank you for having me in today."

"I hope I see you tomorrow," Chico says.

I walk back through the barrio, dodge a few panhandlers, and get on one bus and then another, where I talk the driver into accepting a reduced fare of twenty-five cents for today. My father grants me the time off, so the rest of my week follows the same schedule. I repair nets in the morning and return to the stadium in the afternoon. I work out for Chico every day. At the end of the week, Herb Raybourn will arrive to watch all of us play against the Panamanian National Team. I am sure I will be the last to pitch. Parra is obviously the top prospect here, and there are other guys who have thrown more and gotten a lot more feedback than I have.

I am a bottom-of-the-barrel guy. That much is very clear to me.

And that's fine. I just do whatever they ask. They tell me to go here, and I go here. They tell me to go there, I go there. When they tell me to pitch, I pitch. It never dawns on me that doing well in front of Herb Raybourn is important. I'm not thinking about the future. I can't even imagine it.

On the final day, I ride the same two buses and stop for the same *pan de huevo* and milk. When I get to the stadium, I see Herb talking to Chico. Herb has white hair and a medium build, and his radar gun is ready to go. Like Chico, he is surprised to see me as a pitcher, because he had looked at me as a shortstop, too. I know Herb a little bit. He used to work for the Pittsburgh Pirates and signed several Panamanian big leaguers, including Omar Moreno, Rennie Stennett, and Manny Sanguillen. But mostly I know him because he once signed my cousin Manuel Giron, my mother's nephew. Manuel was also a pitcher, and a lot of people thought he'd be the first player from Puerto Caimito to make the majors. He played three years in the Pirates' system and then got released. He came back to Puerto Caimito and went to work—where else?—in the fishing business. My cousin never talked much about his baseball career, and I didn't ask him. He was back home, which happened to almost everybody, and that was that.

About a half hour before the game, Herb finds me in the dugout.

"You're going to pitch first, so you should warm up," he says.

I am shocked. "I am starting?"

"Yes. I want to put you right out there and show these guys some pitching," Herb says, smiling.

He's got to be kidding, I think.

I get my arm loose and walk out to the mound. Herb settles in behind home plate. I don't know what he's expecting, or what numbers the radar gun will spit out, but I'm not worried about it, either. As inexperienced as I am, I understand pitching enough to know that it involves much more than the miles per hour on your fastball.

The leadoff hitter steps in and I get ahead

on him right away. I settle into a groove quickly, throwing strike after strike, batter after batter. There is no deception to anything I am doing. The ball goes where I want it to, on almost every pitch. The strike zone looks as big as the side of a house. My approach, even then, is to keep it simple.

I go three innings and strike out five and give up one hit. I'm not counting, but I probably don't throw more than thirty or thirty-five pitches, almost all fastballs with one or two very primitive changeups mixed in. When I walk off, Chico shakes my hand.

"Good job, Mariano," he says. "You're done for the day. We're going to look at some of the other guys now."

I thank him and sit in the dugout and watch Parra and the others, wishing I could get out there and play some more, maybe run around the outfield. Not to make an impression. Just to play. I'd always rather play than watch. After the game, Herb asks me if we can talk for a few minutes.

"Of course," I tell him.

"You looked very good out there today," he says. "You made some good hitters look pretty ordinary."

I mumble, "Thank you."

"I think you have a future as a pitcher. I'd like to talk to you and your parents about you signing a contract with the New York Yankees," he tells me. "Can you come here tomorrow and meet me, and then we will go to your house so we can all meet and discuss this?"

"Yes, sure," I tell him, wondering why Herb wants me to meet him at the stadium instead of just driving to Puerto Caimito himself. But I do as he asks. After I get to the stadium, we ride together through the hills and the sliver of rain forest, through Chorrera and finally back to my village. My father is at the boat when we arrive, so I have to go get him. Herb has a small briefcase with him. I wonder what's in it, and wonder what this all means, because it is still not at all clear to me.

When we get to the house, Clara is there,

too, and that's a big comfort. If something important is happening to me, I want her there. Herb opens his briefcase and puts a contract on the table and explains what happens from here, as Clara and my family listen, all of us amazed.

With my parents' blessings, I sign a contract with the New York Yankees. I am getting a $2,000 bonus to be a ballplayer. It is February 17, 1990, a Saturday.

My little marble is about to get a lot bigger.

The New World

Columbus may have had an easier time finding the Americas. My fellow prospect Luis Parra is my traveling companion. We have to change planes in Miami. That means navigating the Miami airport, figuring out where another gate is in a sprawling, crowded airport, and getting there before the plane leaves. Luis is as clueless as I am. It feels as if we've been dropped into the middle of a parade on a distant planet. People are racing around with crazy looks on their faces. Babies are wailing. Announcements are blaring. I've never seen so many people or heard such chaos.

Fortunately, there are enough Spanish-speaking people that, after asking about ten of them for help, we find the gate for the short hop to Tampa. The flight is memorable because I discover, two trips into my career as a frequent flier, that being off the ground terrifies me. I will fly millions of miles in the next twenty-plus years. It never gets better.

The Tampa airport is less hectic but the same amount bewildering. All the signs are, of course, in English.

Bagel? French fries? Home of the Whopper?

What do these things mean?

Baggage claim? Lost and found? Ground transportation?

Can somebody please explain?

Luis and I keep walking. Our goal is to find a guy in a Yankee hat and Yankee jacket. This is all they tell us: "Look for a guy named Chris wearing Yankee stuff. He's sort of a roly-poly guy in his late thirties. You can't miss him."

Actually, we could miss him, very easily. If anybody else is wearing a Yankee hat and jacket, we're in trouble. They probably wouldn't leave No. 1 draft choices who don't speak English to fend for themselves in a strange airport, but we are nobodies, a couple of Panamanian kids who signed for roughly the price of a used car, so no royal treatment for us. We get Chris in his Yankee outfit.

Down the escalator we go, to the baggage carousel.

"*Mira*," I tell Luis, pointing to a guy in a Yankee jacket. "He looks like he's waiting for somebody."

We walk over.

"Chris?" I ask.

He extends his hand. He says several enthusiastic sentences of words. I recognize "Tampa" and "Mariano" and "Luis." That's it. Luis is no help. Neither of us has any idea what he is saying. English isn't our second language. It's not our language at all. Our blank faces tell him as much.

The short trip from the airport to Yankee headquarters blows my mind. The roads are so wide...and so paved. The office buildings and stores are huge and shiny. Everything is dazzling in size and scope, and then we pull into the Yankee complex and get out of the car, and my awe takes off like a speedboat in the Canal.

I look one way and see the most beautifully maintained field I have ever laid eyes on. I look the other way and see another field, just as clean and green, and two more beyond that. How can baseball fields look so perfect? I am guessing the grass is not cut by a kid with a machete.

I am not in El Tamarindo anymore.

There are spotless offices and a spacious clubhouse. There are batting cages and training rooms and more bats and balls and helmets than I knew existed. Chris, who is a clubhouse guy when he isn't an airport driver, hands us practice gear and uniforms. I also get a glove and a set of spikes. It's Christmas in April. We head to the Bay Harbor Inn, a hotel that belongs to Yankees owner George Steinbrenner, where we will live for the season. It's the nicest hotel I've ever stayed in, by far. Here, Luis and I have a television and our own bathroom. We have a stockpile of towels and soaps and shampoos. There is room service, too.

"*¿Qué es el* 'room service'?" Luis asks me.

"*No sé*," I answer. I really have no idea.

Luis and I don't venture far from the hotel very often, because of the language barrier. When we go out to eat, if the server doesn't speak Spanish, we point to the photo on the menu that looks good. Iguana dishes are strangely absent.

When we get on the field and start workouts, I am struck right away by the size of my teammates, the pitchers especially. They are big and a bunch of them are thick-bodied. Our top pitcher, a left-handed kid from Duke University named Tim Rumer, is six foot three and weighs more than 200 pounds. Russ Springer, from Louisiana State University, is six foot four and also 200 pounds, and even a six-foot right-hander from Clemson, Brian Faw, outweighs me by 30 pounds. I watch these guys and wonder if the radar gun will break, they throw so hard. Tim has a curveball that dives about two feet as it crosses the plate.

But the more I practice with the Gulf Coast Yankees, the more I know I can compete with them. When we run and field, I am right there with everybody. And when I am on the mound I discover that, as skinny as I am, and as underwhelming as my 86- or 87-mile-per-hour fastball is, I can do one thing better than just about anybody else:

Put the ball exactly where I want.

With most pitchers in rookie ball, the coaches tell them to just throw strikes, even if they are over the middle of the plate. Once you can do that, you can expand the strike zone and work on fine-tuning your command. But

I have been blessed with the gift of control. If I want to throw the ball knee-high on the black, I do it. If I want to paint the corner, I can do that, too. I still have my one-pitch repertoire—fastball—with a pretty lame slider and a mediocre changeup mixed in. I will work on the changeup for years, and it will never get better. The rookie hitters watch me warm up and probably think, *This is going to be easy.*

Tim Cooper, our third baseman, sometimes catches me in the bullpen. Coop, as we all call him, studied Spanish in high school. He becomes my language instructor. I throw my fastball and he shakes his head. *How are guys not whacking these pitches out of the park every time?* he wonders.

My manager is Glenn Sherlock, and my pitching coach is Hoyt Wilhelm, the old knuckleballer. They are both good guys, though I understand very little of what they say. They put me in the bullpen to start the year. Wilhelm is doing what he can to help, but basically I know nothing about the nuances of pitching. All around me are guys who have been groomed for a decade or more. And then there's me, here because one Sunday afternoon the Panama Oeste Vaqueros needed somebody to bail out a starter who was having a bad day.

But when I get in the game, I am usually ahead of the hitter, 1–2 or 0–2, by the time the announcer finishes saying my name. It goes that way pretty much the whole year. I pitch a total of 52 innings and give up 17 hits and one earned run. I strike out 58 and issue seven walks. My ERA is 0.17. Tim Rumer is the club's pitching star, one of the best in the Gulf Coast League, but with my very average fastball, I have quite a run of success.

This doesn't surprise me.

It shocks me.

All around I see guys who are stronger than me and throw harder than me, and I am outperforming nearly all of them. It is almost an out-of-body experience. I get out after out and think:

How on earth am I doing this?

The way everything is falling together is almost incomprehensible. I should be in the Dominican Republic with the other rookies, not Tampa. Now, in the first few weeks, they see how green I am and start talking about moving me to the DR for extra work, but Herb intervenes.

"Yes, he's raw, but look at the command he has," Herb tells his scouting bosses. "Let's let him pitch in games and see what we've got."

I am getting results that are way beyond my physical abilities. I don't fully understand what is going on. It feels much bigger than me. At night, before I lay my head on the soft pillow at the Bay Harbor Inn, I say a prayer that I can keep it up.

The Anonymous Phenom

Rookie ball is unlike any other level of pro baseball, because it is all new for everybody. For international players like me and Americans who bypass college, it's not just our first time away from home, it's our first time playing this many games—more than sixty—in a season. There is so much to get used to and not everybody figures it out right away. The top pick in the entire big league draft in 1990, Chipper Jones, plays for the Atlanta Braves' Gulf Coast team and hits .229 that year. The premier pitching prospect in the league, José Martinez of the Mets, winds up making a total of four big league appearances. The top reliever, Anthony Bouton of the Gulf Coast Rangers, is out of baseball entirely within two years. Tim Rumer never gets The Call.

I am the twenty-sixth-rated pitcher in the Gulf Coast League. I do not make the All-Star team. I earn $310 every two weeks, after taxes, and save it to give to my parents.

Tim Cooper and I become close friends. I even let him cut my hair. He does a good job, and tutors me in the art of ballplayer humor, too. "I can fix your hair, but I can't do anything about your face," he says. We travel Florida by bus, to Dunedin and Clearwater and Bradenton, and we make a rule: Coop is only allowed to speak Spanish, and I am only allowed to speak English. Some people buy a computer program, like Rosetta Stone, or take a class to learn a new language. I become the student of Tim Cooper, of Chico, California. On the bus, he teaches me words and basic sentences. I pick up more when we go fishing on the wooden pier behind the Bay Harbor Inn. We buy some fishing poles and put our lines in the water. If the fish aren't biting off the pier, we wade into the Gulf of Mexico. Mostly we reel in catfish, which we release. I can't get away from fish no matter where I go.

On a bus trip to Sarasota one day, Coop decides to school me in how to talk to reporters, once we make it to *las Grandes Ligas*.

"Okay, you just won the World Series, and Tim McCarver wants to talk to you," Coop tells me. "You can't call in a translator. That would kill the moment. You have to speak English. Ready?"

I nod.

Coop channels his best Tim McCarver: "Mariano, could you ever have imagined this when you were growing up in Panama— pitching in the World Series for the Yankees?"

"Not really. It's amazing," I tell him. "Thanks to the Lord, I was able to get those last outs."

"You had to face three strong hitters at the end. What was your approach?"

"I just want to make good pitches and get ahead," I tell him.

"You used to work on your father's fishing boat, and now you are a world champion. What have you learned along the way?"

"Dream big," I answer.

Coop ends the interview there. *"Muy bueno,"* he says.

"Thank you, Señor McCarver," I say.

The Gulf Coast Yankees are barely a winning team, but I keep getting people out. With one day left in the season, I have the lowest ERA in the league, but have only pitched a total of forty-five innings—five fewer than a pitcher needs to be eligible for the league ERA title. Sherlock gets permission to let me start against the Pirates so I can get the innings I need, even though I pitched a couple of innings the day before. I haven't gone five innings the whole season, but I figure I can do it if I can keep my pitch count low.

It is August 31, 1990. We have a double-header scheduled at home, in Tampa. I pitch the first game, cruising through four scoreless innings. We take a 3–0 lead. I have not given up a hit as I take the mound in the top of the fifth. A Pirate hitter rips a ball to third base. Coop makes a diving grab, and fires to first to get him. Minutes later in the outfield, Carl Everett, the Yankees' No. 1 draft choice that year, runs down a ball in the gap.

Going into the seventh, the Pirates are still without a hit. They have had one base runner, who reached first on an error. In the minors, doubleheader games are shortened to seven innings, so when I get the first two outs in the seventh, I have only one out to go to pitch a complete-game no-hitter.

All I think is: *Make a good pitch.* I don't let

my mind go anywhere else. I get the guy on a fastball on the corner and an instant later I am engulfed by teammates.

There may be fifty people in the stands, but this moment—and sharing it with my teammates—is one of the best feelings I've ever had on a ball field. It's the first no-hitter I've ever thrown. By the terms of my contract, throwing a no-hitter means an extra $500 and a watch from the Yankees, but do those bonuses apply to a seven-inning game? I call the Yankees player-development office to find out and am assured they do.

In the clubhouse after the game, the Yankees reward our rousing finish by ordering in wings. Coop says, *"Yo creo que me debe un corte de tu bonus para guardar tu no-hitter."* He thinks I owe him a cut of my bonus because he saved my no-hitter with his diving stop at third.

In English, I tell him: "I no understand."

My English still needs work, but I have made great strides in the ballplayer humor department.

I fly to Panama the next day with a completely different outlook than I had five months earlier. I am a pitcher now. A pitcher who wants to compete at the highest level I can. A door has opened to a world of possibilities larger than I have ever imagined. I am not a wannabe mechanic anymore. I am definitely not a fisherman anymore.

I am a professional baseball player.

Climbing the Ladder

During the off-season, I train with Chico Heron at a gym in Panama City. I get up at 5:00 a.m. and take the same two buses I took to the Yankee tryouts at Estadio Juan Demóstenes Arosemena, paying the same $1.10 fare, only now I have enough coins that I don't have to ask the bus driver for credit. I do this five days a week. I lift and run and go through exercise regimens to improve my overall fitness. I throw to build my arm strength. I've seen the competition now, and I know how hard it is for a player to get out of rookie ball. We had thirty-three guys on the Gulf Coast Yankee team. Only seven would make it to the majors, and only five would have careers of any substance: Shane Spencer, Carl Everett, Ricky Ledee, Russ Springer, and me.

If I don't make it, it isn't going to be because somebody outworked me.

I move up to Single-A ball in 1991, pitching for the Greensboro Hornets in the South Atlantic League, splitting time between starting and relieving. It makes no difference to me. I will rake the mound if they want me to. The bigger challenge for me is off the field. I've gotten a good start learning English, thanks to Coop, but unlike Florida, there are not many Spanish speakers in North Carolina. It is tremendously isolating. In restaurants and stores, my inability to express myself is like a brick wall I run into again and again.

I ask somebody for directions one day.

"Excuse me, my English no good, you can tell me how..." I stammer and wobble, and don't manage to say anything. I thought I was beyond this, but my English is getting worse. Another time, I ask a clerk a question about merchandise and receive a blank stare in return. Back at my apartment, I feel more defeated than I have on the field the whole season. It overwhelms me and I cannot stop the tears from coming. I go to the bathroom to wash my face, then turn out the light and try to sleep.

I am still crying.

First thing the next day, I search out Coop. "I need to work on English, Coop," I tell him. "I am not doing good. I have to be able to talk when we win the World Series, right?"

Coop smiles. "We've got a lot of road trips left this year," he says. "You're going to be giving speeches by the time we're done."

I don't give too many speeches, but I don't give up many runs, either. My elbow doesn't feel right all season, honestly, but I don't want anybody to know. No sense jeopardizing my career by complaining about pain that I can manage. I just keep pitching. Thanks to the much-longer road trips in the South Atlantic League, Coop and I have four- and six- and eight-hour bus rides to speak English and Spanish. The extra hours make all the difference. I get comfortable speaking English at last. I am not lost anymore. Tim Cooper is some teammate. Cuts hair, gives language lessons, saves no-hitters. He and I learn an awful lot on those long trips, and not just language.

"If we ever make it to the top, let's make a deal that we're never going to big-league anybody," Coop says. "We're never going to act better than anybody or look down on anybody, because that's not what real big leaguers do."

"That's right," I say. "We don't big-league anybody. We stay humble. We remember where we came from."

"What's important is how you treat people. That's what really matters, right?" Coop says.

"Amen, Coop," I tell him.

My faith in what's important helps me appreciate the moment. Players in the minor leagues always complain about the long hours breathing in diesel fumes, but I can't see it the same way. Without those bus rides, I don't learn English or reinforce the values I want to live by.

I finish the year with a 2.75 ERA and more than a strikeout per inning, even though my win-loss record stinks (4–9). I remain a complete nobody in the orbit of prospects, but you know how much attention I pay to *Baseball America* and its rankings?

None.

When they give me the ball, I take it. I pitch. Most of the time I get people out.

Simple is best.

The Famous Phenom

In the off-season, I marry Clara, the girl of my dreams. Our reception is held at the Fisherman's Hall in Puerto Caimito. What, you were expecting a fancy hotel? No, I am still a fisherman's son from a fishing village.

But all the extra work the Yankees have arranged for me has paid off: I am a better pitcher, and my English has improved as well.

There is just one problem. The pain in my elbow is still there. Despite my trying to ignore it and praying for it to disappear, it gets worse. Our trainer, Greg Spratt, has me keep ice on it all the time. I make sure to warm up properly. But the pain never goes away, and I am left hoping whatever is wrong will heal before next season.

With the wedding behind us, Clara and I begin life together in a tiny room inside her mother's house in Puerto Caimito, a space way smaller than a Little League dugout, with room for a double bed and not much more. Our closet consists of two nails and a broom-stick. Fortunately, we don't have much in the way of clothing. The living is humble even by Puerto Caimito standards, but my plan is to save every penny so we can build our own home. Still, we live with Clara's mother for four years, even after I make the big leagues.

I spend the winter training with Chico again, a regular on the 5:00 a.m. bus, and even as I put in the work, I am so grateful for this man's loyalty and kindness. His reward is seeing me do well. He arranges workouts, helps with mechanics, teaches me how to be a professional—his contributions know no bounds. Whatever I need, Chico Heron provides. You do not forget people like this.

In the spring of 1992, I get promoted to high Single-A ball, the Fort Lauderdale Yankees of the Florida State League. It's not Yankee Stadium, but if you keep moving up a level, it usually means you are still in the mix.

One of my teammates in Fort Lauderdale is Brien Taylor, the No. 1 overall pick in the major league draft in 1991, the Yankees' prize for having their worst record in almost seventy-five years, finishing 67–95, in last place in the American League by a wide margin.

Brien signed for a record bonus of $1.55 million. He is The Future of the Franchise. When Brien warms up, the scene around the bullpen looks like a mall two days before Christmas, crowds clamoring to see the most famous young left arm in baseball. He is mobbed by fans and autograph seekers everywhere we go. His No. 19 jersey is stolen from our clubhouse, a crime that was never solved. Everybody is caught up in Brien Taylor Mania, even Mark Newman, the Yankees minor league boss, who compares his mastery on the mound to Mozart. Other than the $1,548,000 difference in our bonuses, Brien and I are separated by...everything. He is a left-handed African American, a teenager from North Carolina. I am a right-handed Latino, a twenty-two-year-old from southern Panama. He is a prodigy. I am a project. He grew up on the shores of the Atlantic. I grew up on the shores of the Pacific. *60 Minutes* wants to speak to him for a profile. I think *60 Minutes* has lost my phone number. He has a brand-new Mustang with a souped-up sound system. I don't know how to drive.

Still, we connect easily. He strikes me as a down-home country kid, a good teammate, somebody who wants to be one of the guys, even though he's obviously different. I find out how different the first time I see him throw in the bullpen, marveling at his silky motion. He throws 97, 98 miles per hour, and has a big hard curveball, too.

I watch and think: *Wow. This is amazing, the talent this guy has. I have never seen anybody throw a baseball like this.*

Brien is the top-rated prospect in all of baseball, and in his first pro season, straight out of high school, he strikes out 187 batters in just 161.1 innings. His ERA is 2.57. He moves up to Double-A ball the following year, just two rungs on the ladder away from the big leagues. You can imagine him on the mound at Yankee Stadium, blowing away hitters.

Then, a week before Christmas, 1993, I am home in Panama when I see a TV report that Brien has been in some kind of a fight. It doesn't sound like such a big deal, but then the facts come in, something about a brawl at a trailer park in his hometown, and hurting his shoulder.

His left shoulder.

Tell me this is not true, I think.

Brien winds up having surgery, and rehabs through all of 1994. The Yankees bring him back in 1995, to the Gulf Coast League, but his fluid motion, the easy domination, is gone. He has no idea where the ball is going. A year later, he is much worse, walking almost three guys an inning.

I never see Brien again.

The whole thing is so horribly sad. I think about all the fights I got into as a kid. How an injury to my shoulder would have robbed me of a future I didn't even know I had. When I say my prayers, I include Brien, and I thank the Lord for protecting me from doing something stupid in a fit of anger before I even understood what was at stake.

In 1992, the Yankees decide I am a starter. I begin the year well in Fort Lauderdale. The elbow pain is manageable, and if I don't compare to our top pitchers, Brien and Domingo

Jean, I am a pretty fair number three in the rotation. I strike out twelve in one early season victory and follow it with a complete-game shutout of the Fort Myers Miracle. In mid-May, I am named the Florida State League's pitcher of the week. My precision is better than ever—I walk five guys the whole season—and my ERA is just over 2.00, but as the year goes on, troubling signs emerge.

One is that my velocity plummets after I've thrown fifty or sixty pitches. The other is that throwing a slider aggravates the pain in my elbow. It gets bad enough that the Yankees put me on the disabled list in late July.

I stay optimistic, because that is what I do. I'm in my third productive year of pro baseball. There is no reason to panic. I take a break from throwing for a couple of weeks and return in early August against the Dunedin Blue Jays. The Jays have the most dangerous hitter in the league, Carlos Delgado, a twenty-year-old slugger from Puerto Rico. Carlos is on his way to a thirty-home run, one hundred-RBI season, with a .324 average, in the middle of a lineup that also includes Shawn Green, Derek Bell, and Canadian outfielder Rob Butler, who winds up hitting .358, the best in the league.

It's a Friday night in Fort Lauderdale, and I am ready for the challenge of a seriously stacked lineup. I am pitching well, and I move into the fourth inning when the Blue Jays get a man on first. I see him taking a good-sized lead. I fire over to chase him back, but as I do I feel something funny in my elbow. It's hard to describe, but it's not normal.

Definitely not normal.

I catch the return throw and take a moment. My elbow is throbbing. I turn my sights back to the plate and deliver, and now I feel a hard pop in my elbow, as if something just gave out. Or snapped.

Or ruptured.

I get the ball back from the catcher and pause again. I look around the park, fans here and there, maybe a few hundred people in all. They are waiting for the next pitch, and it occurs to me that nobody in the park knows that I am not the same pitcher I was two pitches ago. How could they know? How could they possibly have any clue about what just happened inside my right elbow?

I look the same, but I am not.

I finish the inning, my elbow pulsing with pain. I know I am not going back out there to face Carlos Delgado, or anybody else, any time soon.

"I can't pitch," I tell the manager. "The pain is bad."

The trainer packs my elbow in ice, and I spend the rest of the game on the bench. It is a strange sensation to be out there competing with everything you've got one second, and to be a bystander the next. This is not good.

Will I need surgery? How long will I be out? My head is swirling with questions, but somehow I do not despair. Of course I am concerned about my future. But when the fishing nets were frayed or broken, we fixed them. When the engine on the boat quit, we got ourselves to shore. I come at life from a mechanic's mind-set. If you've got a problem, you figure out what it is and take care of it. That's exactly what I'm going to do with my elbow.

After a bad night of sleep—the elbow is really inflamed and tender—I undergo a series of tests, including an MRI (for "magnetic resonance imaging") in Miami. The MRI does not show damage to my ulnar collateral ligament. The UCL is a thick, triangular band of tissue and the main stabilizing ligament in the elbow. There are more tests, and finally they send me to see Dr. Frank Jobe, the same doctor who would operate on Brien Taylor. He is the king of elbow fixers, the inventor of Tommy John surgery, a term that has become as much a part of baseball vocabulary as grand slam or double play. Elbows don't like throwing thousands upon thousands of baseballs, many at ninety-plus miles per hour. The UCL announces it's had enough by fraying or tearing. Then it has to be rebuilt via surgery—named for the Dodger pitcher who first underwent the procedure—which reconstructs the UCL by knitting it back together with a healthy ligament from another part of your body, usually your forearm.

In Los Angeles, Dr. Jobe provides the diagnosis: I have a lot of wear, and I have stuff floating around in my elbow. To clean up the area will require surgery, which will include the removal of my funny bone, but I don't need a total reconstruction.

I take in Dr. Jobe's words but there is a louder voice talking in my head: *This injury is not going to define me. It is not going to stop me. I will have the surgery I need and do whatever I have to do to get back.*

Dr. Jobe performs my surgery in August 1992, and warns that I may hit some bumps on the road to full recovery. "Don't get discouraged if you don't progress every day. It takes time for the elbow to fully heal. Just be patient," he says.

I am out until the spring of 1993, have a short stay back in the Gulf Coast League, and then join the rotation in Greensboro. I don't have the command I had before, and they have me on a low pitch count, but in ten starts I have an ERA of just over two. It is all coming together, in the halting way Dr. Jobe predicted.

In Greensboro, there's an added bonus of making a new friend, one who will become like a brother to me in the years to come. He's our shortstop, maybe the only guy on the club who is skinnier than me. He was the Yankees' top draft pick the year after they chose Brien Taylor. He is Derek Jeter, of Kalamazoo, Michigan. I had met him before, in minor league camp, but this is the first time we are teammates, and it is some show, because the kid is a year out of high school and all limbs. You are never sure what he will do. I see him inside-out a ball to right-center field and wind up with a triple. I see him rip doubles down the line and hit in the clutch, and play shortstop like a colt in cleats, chasing down grounders and pop flies and making jump throws from the hole.

I also see him throw the ball halfway to Winston-Salem, as if he's still getting used to his six-foot-three-inch body. Derek makes fifty-six errors that season. Years later, we hear stories about how the Yankees were concerned enough that they considered moving him to center field. If anybody had asked my opinion I would have told them not to worry. You could tell already Derek wanted to be great. You could see it in how hard he worked, how passionately he played.

Derek Jeter was going to be just fine.

After the season, there is more medical drama for the Riveras when Clara contracts the chicken pox. Normally, nobody would worry much about chicken pox, but Clara is pregnant with our first child. Chicken pox can be fatal to an unborn baby.

I pray. Clara prays. And this medical odyssey ends well, too. On October 4, 1993, we welcome our first son, Mariano Rivera Jr., into the world in Panama. The father was a little shaky, but mother and child both came through it just fine.

NOTES FROM MO

Finding My Faith

My journey with the Lord does not begin until I am eighteen, working on the fishing boat with my cousin Vidal Ovalle. Vidal and I see each other every day. We chase iguanas together and work together. When I notice a striking change in him, I ask him about it.

"I have come to know the Lord," he says. He shares what he knows about the Bible with me. I can feel his passion, and his peace and happiness. I have known him his whole life, and it's as if he is a different person now. It is not fake. Out at sea, Vidal talks to me about what it means to believe in Jesus Christ.

I listen, and I read the Bible, but I take spiritual baby steps, not quite ready to commit. Years pass. I have unimaginable success pitching in the minor leagues, but life in the United States, away from Clara and my family, is lonely. I lean on the Lord I have come to know through Vidal's help, and through time spent in a small cement church in Puerto Caimito, not far from the dock where my father keeps his boat. It is there I learn to pray, to thank the Lord for his blessings, and seek his forgiveness for my shortcomings.

When I finally am ready to announce in public that I am a Christian, that Jesus is my Savior, it feels like a burden being lifted off my shoulders. I am not alone. The Lord will guide my steps if only I let him. I stand in the front of this tiny church in my tiny village and realize that the Lord is giving me a chance to be a different person, to be joyous. I cannot say no to that.

The Call

The bus trip from Rochester, New York, to Pawtucket, Rhode Island, is seven hours. It seems even longer when you make the trip after getting swept four straight by the Red Wings, the Minnesota Twins' Triple-A team. We pull into Pawtucket late at night, a tired bunch of Columbus Clippers piling into a motel. It's May 1995, and I am off to a strong start with the Yankees' Triple-A team, striking out eleven guys in five and two-thirds innings in my previous game.

We finally win a game to open the series against the PawSox. Tim Rumer gets the victory, and Derek Jeter, hitting .363, knocks a double to put us ahead. Rain postpones the second game of the series. I don't want to spend the whole day in the motel, so I do what minor leaguers usually do when they are on the road: check out the mall. Most malls look almost identical, a Gap here, a Foot Locker there, a food court in the middle, but in Rhode Island, I notice that *everybody* is wearing Boston Red Sox gear.

I'm back in the room that afternoon when the phone rings. It's my manager, Bill Evers, who says, "I have some good news and bad news for you. What do you want first?"

"The bad news," I reply.

"Okay. The bad news is that you are no longer a pitcher for the Columbus Clippers."

¡Ay, no! I spent 1994 moving from Single-A,

to Double-A, and finally to the Clippers. I do not want to reverse course. "What's the good news?" I ask.

"The good news is that you are now a pitcher for the New York Yankees," Bill says.

"Excuse me?"

"You better pack. You're going to New York."

I hear his words the first time. They do not sink in. "Are you serious?" I ask.

"The Yankees want you to get down there as soon as you can," he says. "You need to reach out to the traveling secretary to make the arrangements."

"Okay, thank you very much," I tell him.

"Don't thank me. You earned this," he says.

I hang up the phone. For a long time, I have imagined what it might feel like to get The Call to the big leagues. Now I know.

I stand on the bed and start bouncing up and down, and keep on bouncing, a Panamanian jumping bean. My poor downstairs neighbor. But he won't have to put up with this for long.

I am going to the big leagues.

Las Grandes Ligas.

When I finally stop bouncing, I get on my knees and thank the Lord. Then I call Clara and my parents to share the news—I barely remember what I said—and tell them to let everybody in Puerto Caimito know: Pili is a New York Yankee.

I take a short flight down to New York and get a cab to Yankee Stadium. We are playing a weekend series against the Baltimore Orioles. When I get to the players' entrance, the guard stops me.

"Can I help you?" he asks.

"I'm Mariano Rivera. I just got called up from Columbus," I tell him.

"Okay, we were expecting you," he says.

Expecting me? Imagine that, I think.

It is my first visit to a Major League Baseball stadium. Of course, I have seen major league games on TV, but it's not the same. I catch a glimpse of the field before I walk downstairs to the clubhouse. Even from a distance it looks too big and too beautiful to be real. I meander through a corridor until I find the clubhouse. When I walk in, I see a nameplate over a locker that reads "Rivera," and a No. 42 uniform hanging inside. I wore 58 in spring training, so I guess that makes it official: This really is a promotion.

The whole weekend I am in a pinch-me state, a cartoon version of a typical major league rookie. I have the time of my life in batting practice, shagging fly balls in the most famous outfield in all of baseball. I wish I could stay out there all night, but there is a game to play. The Orioles rally for four in the ninth against John Wetteland to win the opener, but we take the next game, and then get a complete-game, four-hit shutout from Sterling Hitchcock to take the series, before flying to southern California to play the Angels in Anaheim. It is the start of a nine-game, three-city swing. The first game is Tuesday night.

The Yankees' starting pitcher is me.

I am filling in for Jimmy Key, who has gone on the disabled list.

I am more excited than nervous when I get to the ballpark. I've had nine days' rest since my previous start in Rochester, so that should help my shoulder, which hasn't felt great early in the season. No big deal. Just a little cranky. Mel Stottlemyre, our pitching coach, goes over the Angels hitters with me, giving me a brief overview of the best way to attack them. Mel is kind and wise, the sort of man who makes you feel better just being around him. He gives me plenty to digest without giving me too much.

I take my time putting on my uniform—gray road pants and matching jersey—smoothing out the wrinkles. I am so proud to be wearing these clothes and want to be sure they're neat, just the way my school uniform used to be. I head to the bullpen and look up at the three seating decks of the Angels' stadium, the Big A. The size and scope of everything is staggering. I am not so much anxious or in awe as I am incredibly alive. Everything is heightened—the sounds, the smells, the colors. I am minutes away from throwing my first big league pitch.

I am so ready.

The opposing pitcher is Chuck Finley, a hard-throwing left-hander. It's a small crowd on a Tuesday night, and as Tony Phillips, the Angels' leadoff man, settles into the box, I lock in on catcher Mike Stanley's glove. It's as if there is nothing else happening in the entire ballpark, the entire world. All I need to do is hit that glove. This is how all-encompassing my focus is.

I take a breath.

Throw the best pitch you can, I tell myself.

Keep it simple.

I start into my no-windup motion, rocking back slightly, hands by my waist, before I push off the rubber with my right foot. I fire a fastball that runs down and away for a ball, but come back with two strikes on fastballs away and strike out Phillips with another fastball. Jim Edmonds, the center fielder, takes a fastball looking for the second out. Two-thirds of the way done in my first inning in the bigs.

Then Tim Salmon singles to deep short, and Chili Davis, the cleanup hitter, swats a 1–0 pitch for a double. I am in my first jam.

Next up is J. T. Snow, a lefty. I get ahead, 0–2, and then challenge him with a high heater that he lofts to center, where Bernie Williams has an easy play.

Inning over. Phew.

I pitch a scoreless second and get two outs to start the third before Salmon drives a double to right center. I pitch carefully to Davis, remembering his first at-bat, and wind up walking him. Snow hits a weak grounder for an infield hit. Now the bases are loaded and Greg Myers is at the plate. I get ahead, 1–2, but he hits a blooper into left and two runs score.

I get out with no further damage, but remind myself the walk to Davis is what complicated my life and helped put us in a two-run hole.

The trouble starts much sooner in the fourth, with back-to-back singles, bringing up Edmonds. I've struck him out twice, but he battled me the second time and seemed dialed in on my four-seam fastball. I fall behind, 2–1, then leave a pitch over the plate, which he crushes to right-center field. Now it's 5–0, on a night when Finley is making our hitters look like they're swinging with straws. One walk later my debut is history, with a terrible line (three and a third innings, eight hits, five runs, three walks, and five strikeouts) and a disappointing walk to the dugout. We lose, 10–0; Finley strikes out fifteen.

If there's anything positive I can take from this, it's that I know I can get these guys out. It may sound strange after I've been roughed up, but a few pitches in better locations and the whole thing plays out differently. I am ready to make a better showing the next time out.

Five days later, I am back out there again against the Oakland A's. Paul O'Neill belts a double, Bernie Williams homers, and we put up four runs in the first two innings. I protect our lead, pitching one-run ball into the sixth. Bob Wickman bails me out of some minor trouble, and when Wetteland strikes out the side in the ninth, the Yankees have their thirteenth victory of the season and I have the first big league victory of my life. Catcher Jim Leyritz shakes Wetteland's hand after Stan Javier strikes out to end it, and then manager Buck Showalter shakes his hand, and I get in line and do the same. I am so happy to contribute to a victory that I forget to ask for the game ball.

I make two more starts, against the A's and the Mariners. Neither is memorable. I give up a monstrous grand slam in the first game and a three-run homer in the second. The Yankees fall into last place. After the game, Buck Showalter calls me into his office.

I have only three weeks of big league service, but even I know it's not good when you get called into the manager's office, especially when your ERA is 10.20.

"We're sending you back to Columbus," Buck says. "You showed some good things and you shouldn't be discouraged. Just keep working and you'll be back."

As I am leaving the office, Derek Jeter, who was called up two weeks after me, is summoned in. He is hitting .234 in thirteen games, filling in for an injured player. Derek gets the same news: back to the bush leagues. The date is June 11, 1995. The two of us have known nothing but advancement. Going in reverse is not what we have in mind. I know my shoulder is not right, but still...

How can it not sting when your team tells you that you're not good enough?

Derek and I share a very quiet cab ride over

the George Washington Bridge, and then a very quiet meal at a Bennigan's in Fort Lee, New Jersey, across the road from our hotel. It's not the Last Supper, but we're not exactly laughing it up, either.

As much as I know I can compete at the big league level, I am also fully aware that second chances are not guaranteed.

"I feel like it's my fault you got sent down," I tell Derek. "If I had pitched better today maybe this wouldn't have happened—to either of us."

"It's not your fault," Derek says. "What happened to me has nothing to do with the way you pitched. We just have to keep working hard. If we do that and play the way we can, we'll be back."

"You're right. That's how we have to think," I say.

We catch a flight the next morning to Charlotte, where we join the Clippers. My shoulder still feels sore, so I am put on the disabled list for two weeks to see if the rest helps.

My first start back in Triple-A comes on a damp night at Cooper Stadium in Columbus. I am pitching the second game of a double-header against Rochester. Even as I warm up I can tell that my shoulder feels better than it has all year. I am almost pain-free, throwing freely.

The rest has helped. Big-time.

I smoke through the Red Wings in the first inning. In the dugout, my catcher, Jorge Posada, sits next to me. "What did you eat today?" he wants to know.

"Why?"

"Because I've never seen you throw this hard. The ball is flying out of your hand."

"The rest helped. I feel good," I reply.

I wind up throwing a rain-shortened, five-inning no-hitter. I walk one guy, and Jorge throws him out stealing, so I face the minimum fifteen batters.

"This guy is going back to the big leagues

and he is never coming back," Jorge says to a couple of our teammates.

Jorge tells me later that I was at 96 miles per hour all night and might've touched 97 or 98. It is a major jump that stuns people in the Yankee organization. Years later, I find out that Gene Michael, the Yankees general manager, got bulletins that night about how hard I was throwing.

Michael wanted to know, "Was the radar gun working right? Do we know if this is accurate?"

He checked with a scout who confirmed it; his gun registered 96, too. Michael apparently was in the middle of talks with the Tigers to acquire David Wells. The Tigers were interested in me.

Once Michael confirmed the accuracy of the radar readings, I was no longer in that deal.

The night after my abbreviated no-hitter, Jorge and I and some of the other Clippers go to our regular dinner spot, Applebee's. I have filet mignon, a loaded baked potato, and vegetables.

"Do you have any idea how you could go from throwing eighty-eight to ninety to ninety-six?" Jorge asks.

My shoulder is healthy, but there is only one answer that suits the way I really feel about this. "It is a gift from God," I tell Jorge.

I never pitch for the Columbus Clippers again.

NOTES FROM MO

The House That Ruth Built

Not so long ago, I asked, "Who's Babe Ruth?" Now here I was, playing in his house. "The House That Ruth Built" is what the sportswriters called the original Yankee Stadium, because it was Ruth's enormous popularity that made a new home for his team necessary.

Before the Stadium opened in the Bronx in 1923, the Yankees had, for ten years, shared the Polo Grounds in Manhattan with one of the city's two National League teams, the Giants.

But in 1920, the Yankees acquired Ruth from the Boston Red Sox, where he had made a name for himself as a batter, even though he had come up as a pitcher. In 1919, Ruth broke the American League record by hitting twenty-nine home runs, nearly doubling the previous record of sixteen, set by Socks Seybold of the Philadelphia Athletics in 1902.

In his first year with the Yankees, Ruth hit *fifty-four* home runs, and his big swing and even bigger personality drew 1.3 million Yankee fans to the Polo Grounds, surpassing the Giants' attendance. Suddenly, the Giants' owner wasn't so sure he wanted to share his ballpark with an American League team, and suggested the Yankees find another place to play their home games.

The Yankee owners bought ten acres of land, a former lumberyard, on the Harlem River, and built the country's first three-deck stadium. At the time, ballparks typically seated about 30,000 fans; Yankee Stadium could house nearly 60,000.

The opening of the Stadium coincided with the beginning of the Yankees' winning history. Though they had never won a pennant or the World Series before, once Ruth joined the team, the Yankees won seven American League championships and four World Series titles. Appropriately, the first home run hit at Yankee Stadium came during an opening-day victory over the Red Sox—a three-run dinger hit by, you guessed it, The Babe.

Back in the Bigs

The next time the manager of the Clippers calls to tell me I'm rejoining the Yankees, I don't jump up and down on the bed. I just get on a plane to Chicago. I am starting the next day against the White Sox. From the moment I walk into Comiskey Park, I am at peace. I just want to go out there and play the game I love. Already I am learning that when you tell yourself, *I have to do this* or *I must prove myself right now*, you just make it harder for yourself.

I can't say that I know I am throwing that much harder than I was in my previous call-up, but I can tell by how hitters are swinging that I am bringing it and they are not expecting it. I cruise through four innings with one hit and five strikeouts. Paul O'Neill belts a homer to give me a 1–0 lead, and a sacrifice fly plates another run to make it 2–0.

After six innings, I have given up only two hits. I strike out the side in the seventh.

With a 3–0 in the eighth, I get the first batter to bounce out, the next to pop out, and the third on a strikeout. It is my eleventh strikeout of the night. When I reach the dugout, Buck Showalter pats me on the back.

"Great job, Mariano. You were tremendous," he says. "I'm going to give the ball to Wetteland for the ninth."

"Thank you," I say. Somebody tells me later that the Sox hitters complained because the scouting reports they got on me were wrong. The reports said I threw in the mid- to high eighties, not the mid-nineties.

Well, those reports are a few weeks out-of-date.

I stay with the big club the rest of the season, and we clinch the first American League wild-card by winning eleven of our last twelve games, drawing the Seattle Mariners in the division series. It's a joyful time to be a Yankee. This isn't just the first postseason series for the Yankees in fourteen years, it's the first playoff series ever for the great Don Mattingly, and everybody is thrilled for him. I have only known Donnie for a few months, but it's long enough to admire his humility and his work ethic. He is a man who does everything the right way.

He is a man you want to be like.

We win Game 1 at Yankee Stadium behind David Cone. Game 2 is tighter, tied 4–4 after nine innings. Before the top of the twelfth, a call goes to the bullpen.

"Get Rivera up."

I get loose, feeling good. I like the way the ball is coming out of my hand.

Ken Griffey Jr. hits a home run to give the Mariners a 5–4 lead. When Wetteland walks the next hitter, Buck calls for me. I run in from the bullpen for the biggest pitching test of my life. I am a fisherman's son from Puerto Caimito, but I love the high stakes, love that so much is riding on every pitch. I can't wait.

Maybe it comes from working on the boat. If we don't catch any fish, we don't make any money. We have to come through.

The playoffs feel the same way to me.

I strike out Jay Buhner, the former Yankee, to end the threat.

In the bottom of the twelfth, we are down to our final out when Rubén Sierra rips a double to left to tie the game, and now it's up to me to hold it. I have an easy thirteenth inning and strike out the side in the fourteenth. I get Griffey to fly out, retiring eight straight batters, before giving up singles in the fifteenth to Edgar Martínez and Buhner. I strike out Doug Strange but now fall behind Tino

Martinez, 3–0, with two men on. I throw a fastball and he hits a fly ball to center.

Threat extinguished.

My first postseason outing consists of three and one-third innings of scoreless relief.

Minutes later, with one man on and one man out in the bottom of the fifteenth, Yankee Jim Leyritz rocks a two-run homer into the right-center-field bleachers, and as I watch its flight from the dugout and listen to the roar that goes up, I think only one thing:

This is the loudest noise I've ever heard in my life.

It feels as if the Stadium is lifting off River Avenue. We are up two games to none, and I get the victory. It is hard to even comprehend where I am, and what I am doing.

The series moves to Seattle, and the Mariners take the third and fourth games. In the eighth inning of Game 5, after the last of David Cone's amazing 147 pitches, a ball four forces in a run to tie it. Buck gives me the ball. The bases are loaded and Mike Blowers is at the plate.

Four months earlier, I was a Columbus Clipper who had washed out in his big league audition. Now I have the outcome of an entire postseason series riding on my every pitch. The pressure is immense, but this is no time to think about how fast, or how far, I've come. I have a hitter to get out. I lock in on Mike Stanley's glove.

I strike out Mike Blowers on three pitches.

We wind up losing in the eleventh inning, when Edgar Martínez doubles in the winning run. It is a brutal ending, an ending I never see coming. My insides go cold watching the Mariners celebrate right in front of us. I was sure we would win this series, that we would be doing the dancing. But along with the sting, there is also a resolve that borders on defiance: We will learn from this. We will be back. We will prevail.

And it's impossible for me not to feel heartened by what happens in 1995. After all, I begin the year as a question mark with a shaky history of injury, a Triple-A pitcher all

the way. I finish it with five and a third scoreless innings and eight strikeouts in postseason
competition for the New York Yankees, in *las
Grandes Ligas*, playing a game I learned on a
beach.

World-Class

I have a new pitching home in 1996, and I spend the next 1,096 appearances of my career there. It's called the bullpen. I guess if you put me against a wall and force me to answer, I'd say I'd prefer to start, but whatever the club needs, I will do my best.

It's a season of major transition for the Yankees. We have a new manager, Joe Torre; a new ace, Andy Pettitte; a new shortstop in Derek Jeter; a new first baseman, former

Mariner Tino Martinez; and a new catcher—
a smart, solid guy named Joe Girardi. You
never know how it will actually piece together,
and I guess George Steinbrenner isn't so sure
himself: The Yankees are talking to the Mariners about trading me for their shortstop,
Felix Fermin. Apparently, Steinbrenner is
unsure that Derek is ready and wants Fermin
as an insurance policy. I have no clue the talks
are going on, and don't want to know. Some
players want to be on top of every last trade
rumor. Not me. Rumors are a distraction, and
in my worldview as a pitcher, distractions are
the enemy.

If it's not going to help me get outs, why
pay attention?

My main focus is to make a strong first
impression on the new manager. I have never
heard of Joe Torre, know nothing of his playing career or his MVP award. Buck Showalter,
my previous manager, was a big supporter of
mine. When the Yankees decide to let Buck go
and bring in Mr. T—it's what I call him even

now—I get fired up to win a bullpen spot. There are a lot of relievers in camp. Though I did well in the playoffs the year before, I take nothing for granted.

In my first outing of the regular season, I throw two scoreless innings against the Rangers. It's almost embarrassing, but I still basically have a repertoire of one pitch: a four-seam fastball. Years trying to develop a slider and changeup have yielded no breakthrough. It doesn't seem to matter. I have easy heat with late movement, and usually can put it exactly where I want.

Six weeks into 1996, I have an ERA of 0.83. At one point, I throw fifteen straight no-hit innings. During a midseason hot streak in which we win eight of nine, I strike out three Red Sox on twelve pitches, while getting the hold for Wetteland. Soon there is some clamor that I should be named to Mike Hargrove's All-Star staff. Hargrove passes on me, and if Yankee fans get all worked up about it, I don't. I'm just not wired that way.

All I want to do is get home to Panama during the All-Star break to see Clara, who is pregnant with our second son, Jafet.

I finish the year with a 2.09 ERA and 130 strikeouts in 107 innings; I even finish third in the Cy Young voting for the league's best pitcher. We win the American League East and draw the Rangers in the division series. The Rangers win Game 1 at Yankee Stadium, so it makes the second game crucial, if we want to avoid going to Texas having to sweep.

Andy pitches into the seventh and then I get the ball. We are down, 4–2. I face eight Rangers in all, and get all eight of them, including Juan González, the league's Most Valuable Player that year. He already has two homers and four RBIs in the game, and three homers for the series. González is in one of those zones hitters get into—when the ball looks as big as a cantaloupe, and they don't *think*, they *know*, that they can hit anything. Pitchers get in zones, too, and I am in one myself. González hit a homer off me the year before, so I know how dangerous he can be. Unlike most sluggers, he almost always makes contact against me; I struck him out only one time in twenty-four career at-bats. He is a very good low fastball hitter, so I keep the ball up and away. That works: I get him to ground out to lead off the eighth.

We wind up tying the game in the eighth on Cecil Fielder's single, and winning it in the twelfth after Derek smacks a leadoff hit and scores on a bad throw. Series tied 1–1.

We have been a resilient team all season, never quitting, and we demonstrate it again in Game 3, in Texas, when we're down a run in the ninth and score twice to win the game.

One game later, I throw two more scoreless innings as we take a 5–4 lead into the ninth. Bernie Williams hits his second homer of the game, and Wetteland whiffs Dean Palmer to take the series.

We move into the American League Championship Series against the Baltimore Orioles, and right away fall behind by two runs. We are still trailing in the eighth when Derek hits a deep fly ball to right field. The Orioles outfielder Tony Tarasco goes back to the wall and lines up to make the catch. The ball falls into the outstretched mitt of...Jeffrey Maier. Never heard of him? He is twelve years old at the time, a seventh grader from Old Tappan, New Jersey. Always bring your glove to the game, kids. No, it isn't a legitimate home run, and yes, the Orioles have every right to argue, but these are the days before home runs can be video-reviewed by the umpires.

The game is still tied when I get a ground out to escape a jam in the tenth, and strike out to end the eleventh. Three minutes later, Bernie wraps a 1–1 pitch around the left-field foul pole to seal a 5–4 victory. The Stadium erupts in pandemonium. In the outfield, fans are chanting Jeffrey Maier's name and the letters *MVP*.

The Orioles square the series at one by taking Game 2, and then we head to Camden Yards, where Jimmy Key pitches a masterpiece in Game 3. In Game 4, our bullpen—David Weathers, Graeme Lloyd, me, and Wetteland— throws six shutout innings after Kenny Rogers is knocked out early. We go up, 3–1. Andy finishes off the Orioles in Game 5 by pitching three-hit ball over eight innings, and Jim Leyritz, Fielder, and Darryl Strawberry all homer in a six-run third off Scott Erickson to put us into the World Series against the Atlanta Braves.

You'd think that being in my first World Series would bring a whole new level of pressure, but the way our year went, we expected to be in the Series. If we had fallen short, that would've been crushing, so the pressure actually felt greater in the playoffs.

You never would know that by the way the Series begins, though, with the Braves playing the role of tractor and the Yankees playing the role of dirt clump. We lose two games at home by a combined score of 16–1, mostly because Andruw Jones, a nineteen-year-old from Curaçao, an island off the coast of Venezuela, crushes two homers in Game 1, and the Braves' starting rotation—one of the best ever—is as good as everybody says. John Smoltz shuts us down in the first game, Greg Maddux in the second. I am in awe watching these guys, especially Maddux. He throws eighty-two pitches in eight innings, going to a three-ball count on only two batters. In the fourth inning, he sets down the heart of our order on six pitches. He does what great artists in every line of work do.

He makes it look easy.

The Series switches to Atlanta, and we win Game 3 behind David Cone, but we are in big trouble late in Game 4, down 6–3—five outs from being down three games to one, and having to face Smoltz and Tom Glavine in the next two games. I am getting loose in the bull-pen as the eighth inning begins, with Charlie Hayes leading off against Mark Wohlers, one of the most dominant closers in the game.

Hayes hits a swinging bunt that teeters along the third-base line and somehow stays fair. Then Darryl Strawberry rips a line drive and we have two runners on, nobody out. I am still warming up when Mariano Duncan hits a double-play ball to short but Rafael Belliard bobbles it and gets only one out.

That brings up Jim Leyritz, who'd hit that huge homer against the Mariners the previous October, and homered in the clinching game against the Orioles. Leyritz has never faced Wohlers before.

"What's Wohlers got?" Leyritz asks Rick Down, the hitting coach.

"He's got a hundred-mile-per-hour fast-ball," Down says.

Leyritz steps in, using one of Strawberry's bats. He fouls one off, then takes a slider for a ball. On the 1–1 pitch, Wohlers throws another slider, up and over the plate, and Leyritz drives it deep to left. Andruw Jones climbs the wall, but the ball is beyond his reach. The game is tied, and as Leyritz fist-pumps his way around the bases, I know it's on me to make sure it stays that way.

I pitch a scoreless eighth, and get one out in the ninth. Graeme Lloyd picks me up, getting Fred McGriff to hit into a double play. We win it in the tenth. Series tied 2–2.

In Game 5, Andy Pettitte and John Smoltz both pitch brilliantly, but we take a 1–0 victory and head back to Yankee Stadium with a 3–2 Series lead. We finally get to Maddux with three runs in the third, and we still have a 3–1 lead when I come in, in the seventh inning. I plow through two innings, retiring six straight after walking Terry Pendleton to open the seventh, before turning the ball over to Wetteland. He gives up three singles and a run and the Braves have the tying run on second when the Braves second baseman, Mark Lemke, pops up in foul territory behind third, where Charlie Hayes catches it.

The World Series is ours.

From the top step of the dugout, I sprint to the mound, arriving almost before Charlie lands from his jump. It's the Yankees' first championship in eighteen years, and my first World Series title ever. For three guys from the Columbus Clippers—Derek, Andy, and me—to play such important roles in the victory makes it that much sweeter. To be in that pile and celebrate after we had to come back to beat a team as good as the Braves is an indescribable feeling.

NOTES FROM MO

Thanks, Jeff!

The sportswriters pretty much agreed on two things about Game I against the Orioles. One: Fan interference should have been called. Umpire Rich Garcia admitted later that he blew the call, and after the season, the Yankees installed a railing behind the right-field fence to prevent fans from reaching over it. Two: Young Jeffrey Maier had very good instincts as an outfielder.

Jeff shot out of his seat at the crack of the bat and hustled to the exact spot on the rail where the ball would end up. "The ballplayer in me just took over," he told reporters. He had brought his black Mizuno outfielder's glove with him because, "It's what every kid wants to do at a ball game—catch a ball."

Jeff became instantly famous: He was on *Good Morning America* the next day and the *New York Daily News* gave his family tickets behind the Yankees dugout to Game 2. And Jeff grew up to be a very good baseball player himself. He played for his high school team and set the all-time record for hits at Wesleyan University in Connecticut. He had several tryouts with major league teams but never caught fire in the minors.

One lasting disappointment is the lack of his rightful souvenir. After he caught Jeter's ball, another fan "ripped the glove right off my hand," he said. He lost the ball in that moment.

The Cutter

After the season, the Yankees decide I am ready to be their closer and let Wetteland, a free agent, sign with the Rangers. Publicly, I insist I feel no pressure, but the truth is that (finally) I *do* feel pressure. I want to prove that the Yankees did the right thing; I don't want to be as good as John Wetteland. I want to be better.

We start the 1997 season by winning only five of our first fifteen games. I blow three of my first six save opportunities. In my first nine innings, I give up fourteen hits and four runs.

The most recent slipup comes against the Angels, and the guy who gets me is Jim Leyritz, of all people. Traded six weeks after his homer against the Braves, Leyritz whacks a two-run double down the left-field line. After the game, Mr. T calls me into his office. Mel Stottlemyre, the pitching coach, is there. I'm pretty sure they don't want to talk about where to go for dinner. I haven't been doing the job. If it keeps up this way, they'll have to make a change.

"I'm not sure what's wrong," I tell them. "I feel good but I'm not getting the results."

Mr. T says, "Mo, know what you need to do? You need to be Mariano Rivera. Nothing more, nothing less. It looks to us like you're trying to be perfect."

"You've gotten away from what made you so successful," Mel says. "By trying to do too much, you're taking away some of your aggressiveness and hurting your command."

"You are our closer. You are our guy, and we want you to be our guy, and that is not going to change, okay?" Mr. T says.

I feel an immediate sense of relief. I look both of them in the eye, first Mr. T, and then Mel. "Thank you," I say. "Knowing you still have faith in me means so much."

In sports, trying too hard to succeed is almost the surest way to fail. Joe and Mel are exactly right. I still have the same arm, the same stuff, but pushing myself to be better or faster than I was before is hurting me. Sometimes you have to just let your body do what it does naturally.

As I walk out of Mr. T's office, I feel 10,000 tons lighter. I make a vow to remember what he told me. And I devise my own little trick to help: I am not going to think about what inning it is. Whether it's the seventh or eighth inning, the way it was a year ago, or the ninth inning, the way it is this year, I still have a ball, the hitter still has a bat, and my only job is to get him out, one pitch at a time.

I've had a great deal of success since the end of 1995 in getting hitters out. So why change anything? That's what I need to keep in mind.

The payoff from the meeting is immediate. I stop trying to be Wetteland and run off twelve straight saves. By the time we head into Tiger Stadium for a series in late June, the insecurities are behind me.

Who had any idea what would be ahead of me?

I am playing catch with Ramiro Mendoza, fellow pitcher and fellow Panamanian, before the game. As I get loose, I start to throw a bit harder. I catch Ramiro's throw and, heating up now, fire it back to him.

My throw surprises him. He has to move his glove at the last moment to catch it.

"Hey, stop playing around," Ramiro says.

"What are you talking about?" I ask.

"I'm talking about the ball you just threw. It almost hit me."

"I just threw a normal ball," I say.

"Well, it didn't look normal to me."

We keep playing catch. I throw the ball to him again and the same thing happens. It breaks about a foot right when it reaches him, and again he almost misses catching it.

"That's what I'm talking about," he says. "Stop doing that."

"I promise I am not doing anything," I reply.

I make several more throws to Ramiro and every one of them has the same wicked movement at the end.

"You better go find somebody else to catch you," he says finally. "I don't want to get hurt."

He's serious. Our game of catch is over.

I have no idea what just happened, and no idea why the ball is moving this way. I am not aware of doing anything different. I head to the bullpen, which is on the field at old Tiger Stadium, and throw to our bullpen catcher, Mike Borzello. My ball—what I think is my regular four-seam fastball—is doing the same thing that it did with Ramiro.

"Whoa! Where did that come from?" Borzi asks. He's sure something is wrong with the baseball—that it has a scuff that's making it move this way. He throws it aside and gets a new ball.

The same thing happens. Borzi holds up his hands. "What's going on? What are you doing?" he asks.

"I don't know. I am just throwing my regular four-seam fastball," I say, showing him my grip.

Mel Stottlemyre joins the conversation and watches me throw. He looks at my grip, my arm angle, everything. I cannot throw this pitch straight.

For several weeks, we fiddle with my grip and release point but the ball keeps moving late, boring in on left-handed hitters and away from righties. As we tinker, I continue to pitch, and the more I throw this new pitch, the more command I get of it. I am throwing it for strikes.

I realize it's absurd to try to throw the ball straight. What pitcher wants *less* movement on the ball?

This is how my cut fastball, or cutter, is born. It's as if it dropped straight from heaven, as if I were on my father's boat and a million fish just swam into our nets, the radar gone a deep, deep red. I don't spend years searching for this pitch. I don't ask for it, or pray for it. All of a sudden it is there, a devastating weapon. I am throwing the ball across the seams with the slightest bit of additional pressure, and my fastball now has this wicked tail. How does this happen? I don't know.

But it changes my whole career.

By midseason, I have twenty-seven saves and a 1.96 ERA. Mr. T names me to the All-Star team. The game is played at Jacobs Field in Cleveland. I come into the ninth with a 3–1 lead, thanks to a two-run homer by the

Indians' Sandy Alomar Jr. and a solo blast from Edgar Martínez. I am very happy to have Edgar on my team rather than having to pitch to him. This guy owns me. He has a .312 career batting average against all pitchers but a .579 average against me. I start the ninth by striking out Charles Johnson, then get Mark Grace to ground out and Moises Alou to line out, getting in and getting out, my favorite kind of save.

We have one of the best records in baseball after the break, but still finish two games behind the Orioles. As the wild-card team, we earn a division series matchup against Cleveland. It opens in the Bronx, and a traffic jam around the Stadium hasn't even cleared by the time the Indians have scored five times against David Cone. A walk, a hit-by-pitch, a wild pitch, three singles, and Sandy Alomar Jr.'s three-run homer make for a big mess.

But, just as in our championship run the year before, we refuse to surrender.

Ramiro Mendoza pitches three and a third superb innings in relief of Cone, and we start our charge. Tino Martinez homers, and we scratch out another run to chase Orel Hershiser out of the game. In the sixth, Tim Raines, Derek, and O'Neill pound out consecutive homers to put us up 8–6. Jeff Nelson holds them into the eighth, then I get four outs, striking out Matt Williams to end it.

Tino, who had a monster regular season, keeps it up in Game 2, drilling a two-run double in a three-run first. With Andy pitching, I figure our lead will hold up, but the Indians score five times with two outs in the fourth, and by the time Williams takes Andy deep for a two-run shot an inning later, Cleveland is on its way to a 7–5 victory.

In these tight best-of-five series, the third game is always pivotal, and it couldn't go any better as the series shifts to Cleveland, thanks to a grand slam from Paul O'Neill and a brilliant outing from David Wells. We cruise, 6–1, and, now just a victory away from the ALCS, we get a solid start from Dwight Gooden and take a 2–1 lead into the eighth. Mike Stanton strikes out David Justice looking, and then Mr. T gives the ball to me to get the last five outs. I get Matt Williams on a flyout. The next hitter is Alomar.

I fall behind, 2–0. I don't want the tying run at first, so there's no way I am going to walk him. But I'm not going to just throw something down the middle to get a strike. Joe Girardi sets up away. I am looking to hit the outside corner, low. I fire a cutter. The ball is out over the plate, almost shoulder height. I miss my spot badly. The pitch is ball three.

I am surprised when Alomar swings.

I am shocked when he hits it into the first row in the right-field seats.

The game is tied. The Cleveland fans erupt. The Indians win in the bottom of the ninth and take Game 5 to end our reign as world champions much sooner than any of us expected.

NOTES FROM MO

Learning from Mistakes

Giving up the homer to Sandy Alomar Jr. is the greatest failure of my young career. I know my coaches are concerned about how I am going to handle it. A small mistake in a big situation can get into the head of an athlete and do significant damage. Mark Wohlers is never the same pitcher after Leyritz's home run in the 1996 World Series. Other relievers have responded similarly after blowing key save situations.

But almost the minute Alomar's ball sails over Paul O'Neill's glove, I know that not only is this not going to break me, it is going to make me better.

I learn from that pitch. If you watch the replays closely, you can see I don't finish correctly, and leave my release point too high. I'm not sure if I gave Sandy a hundred more pitches in the same spot that he would hit another one out, but the point is that I have to finish that pitch properly, have to be so focused, have to be so completely consistent with my mechanics that I do not miss my spot by so much.

Of all the talents an athlete can have, maybe the most important one is the ability to focus. I am not easily distracted or deterred or discouraged. I cannot bring back Sandy Alomar's homer. I can't change the outcome of the division series. But I do know that I hate the feeling that I have when I walk off the mound that night in Jacobs Field. And I am going to do all I can to make sure it doesn't happen again.

Shades of '27

I start 1998 with a blown save and a trip to the disabled list, thanks to a strained muscle. We lose four of our first five games, but not much more goes wrong the rest of the year.

The 1927 Yankees, long considered one of the best baseball teams in history, won 110 games with a batting lineup nicknamed "Murderers' Row" that included Babe Ruth—I know who he is now—who hit sixty home runs.

The 1998 Yankees win *114* games, scoring the most runs in the league while allowing the fewest earned runs. The staff ERA of 3.82 is a full run better than the league average. I wind up with thirty-six saves, a 1.91 ERA, and a total of thirty-six strikeouts—the lowest number for any full year of my career. This is by design. Mel Stottlemyre is concerned that strikeouts will run up my pitch count, and I might run out of gas by the postseason. In 1997, for example, when I struck out a batter an inning, I threw 1,212 pitches. A year later, with better results, I throw three hundred fewer pitches.

Would Sandy Alomar Jr. have hit that homer if my arm had been fresher? Would my cut fastball have had a little more bite on it?

"Why not save the wear on your arm?" Mel suggests.

"Sounds good to me," I say.

With my cutter getting sharper, I am breaking more bats, but getting fewer strike-outs. When I was learning to pitch, I'd go up the ladder—a fastball at the thighs, one at the waist, and then one chest-high. Batters would chase the high one and miss. But hitters adjust. When they realize they can't touch the 96- or 97-mile-per-hour fastball up in the zone, they lay off. You have to find another way to beat them. And for me, that way is the cutter.

We wrap up the regular season twenty-two games ahead of the second-place Red Sox.

There are wacky numbers all over baseball that year, especially in the home run department. Mark McGwire and Sammy Sosa are chasing baseball history, trying to break the record of sixty-one homers in a season set by the Yankees' Roger Maris in 1961. (He broke the record set by—there's that name again—Babe Ruth.) McGwire will finish with seventy, Sosa with sixty-six, and there are a slew of other guys right behind them. I don't think anything of it at the time, but I am totally naive when it comes to steroids. I'm not saying that everybody among the home run leaders used performance-enhancing drugs, though a number of them later admitted as much. I'm just saying that I could've stepped on a pack of syringes and not known what was going on. Not only have I never taken any steroids, I've never seen anybody else take them, either.

The Yankees spend a phenomenal 152 consecutive days in first place, but that still means taking care of business every single day. As I approach my thirtieth birthday, I understand more than ever that preparing properly is everything.

I am a person who likes order and finds comfort in routine, especially on game days. After I shag flies during batting practice, I grab something to eat, usually chicken or pasta. Occasionally, we order from Popeyes. (I can't lie about this. There are delivery boys out there who brought fried chicken to Yankee Stadium and told the security guards, "I have an order for Rivera....")

Once nourished, I am in the hot tub before the first inning starts. I submerge myself to get my body good and loose. After fifteen minutes, I towel off, stretch, and, if necessary, have the therapist massage any tightness in my muscles. I get dressed very methodically, then head to the trainer's room, typically at the start of the fourth inning, where Gene Monahan stretches my arm and legs some more. All the while, I am paying close attention to the game on TV, studying the opposing hitters' at-bats, looking for tendencies or possible weaknesses.

This time with Geno is probably my favorite part of the day, outside of being on the mound. It is unhurried. Geno and I talk about our families and what's going on in the world. It brings closure to my preparation. By the time I leave his training table, I can almost feel my adrenaline starting to surge. I head for the bullpen in the middle or the end of the sixth, ready to compete. On a Sunday in early August at the Stadium, I stick to the routine religiously, throw a scoreless inning against the Royals for my thirtieth save, and lower my ERA to 1.25. It raises our record to 84–29, and by the time our nine-game winning streak is over, we are 89–29.

With the way we've dominated all year, we're huge favorites to win the World Series, a status that can bring its own pressure. The Rangers are our first-round opponent, but their heavy hitters are no match for our pitchers. They score one run in three games and we sweep. I pitch in all three games, getting two saves, giving up one hit. Then it's on to a rematch with the Indians.

After we take the opener behind David Wells, the Indians win two straight, and now we're looking at the biggest game of our season. A loss and we're in a 3–1 hole. Orlando Hernández—we call him El Duque—is brilliant in his first postseason start, throwing three-hit ball over seven innings in a 4–0 victory to tie the series at two-all. But to avoid facing an elimination game in Jacobs Field, we need to win Game 5, too.

Wells is superb for the second time in the series, striking out eleven and pitching into the eighth. I come on with one out and a 5–3 lead, the tying runs on base. So here I am again in an eighth inning at Jacobs Field, in Year 1 After Alomar.

At the plate is the Indians' left fielder Mark Whiten, who had been on our side in this series the year before. Hard Hittin' is what Whiten likes to be called. It's the biggest at-bat of the game, if not the series. The count goes to 2–2, and I bring a hard cutter that tails in on him. Whiten hits a weak grounder to second for a double play that ends the threat.

An inning later, I get three quick outs to put us one game away from the World Series.

David Cone, a twenty-game winner, starts Game 6, and Scott Brosius clobbers a three-run homer. We jump to a 6–0 lead. A party atmosphere is building in Yankee Stadium, but then Jim Thome hits a grand slam and the Indians pull within one. Mendoza, the teammate who won't play catch with me, gives us three brilliant innings of relief, and Derek hits a two-run triple for some much-needed breathing room.

I come in for the ninth with an 8–5 lead. Nine pitches later, I grab Omar Vizquel's comebacker, toss it to Tino, and we're heading back to the Series. The guys mob me, and the joy I feel is deep. I am not big on redemption. It's not as if I go out there consciously thinking I have to make up for the Alomar home run. I believe that being fully committed to the present, without any worries about the past, is the best attribute a closer can have. You wonder why the shelf life of so many short relievers is, well, so short? Why guys can be unhittable for a year or two and then disappear? It's because it takes a ton of concentration, and self-belief, to not let the highs and lows mess with your head. Twelve months After Alomar, I pitch in four of the five games against the Indians, and don't allow a hit. I strike out five. My ERA is 0.00.

I am ready for the San Diego Padres, and the World Series, and for an interesting family subplot, too. My cousin Rubén Rivera is a Padre. Rubén is four years younger than me, a power-hitting center fielder with the sort of physique and skills that make scouts feel faint. But Rubén is one of those young guys who is a little too taken with the fame that comes with being a gifted big league player. He wants to be a star yesterday, and when it doesn't happen on his timetable, he gets frustrated. Rubén winds up moving ten times in his big league career. I always wanted him to find a stable situation in the big leagues so that he could relax and let his gifts shine, but it never really happened for him until he got to Mexico, where he became one of that league's top sluggers.

I want all the best for Rubén. After we win four games against his team, of course.

David Wells gets the ball again, but this time he's outpitched by Padres ace Kevin Brown, who takes a 5–2 lead into the bottom of the seventh. When Brown gives up a hit and a walk to start the eighth, Bruce Bochy, the Padres' manager, calls for reliever Donne Wall, who immediately gives up a three-run homer to Chuck Knoblauch. Before the inning is over, Tino hits a grand slam and we've scored seven runs. This is how it has gone all year. Production comes from everywhere. We have a No. 9 hitter, Scott Brosius, with 19 homers and 98 RBIs. We have Jorge Posada, a switch-hitting catcher in his first full year, hitting 17 homers and knocking in 63 runs, also at the bottom of the order. I come on in the eighth and get a four-out save.

The Padres' problems deepen when we score seven more times in the first three innings of Game 2. With our Cuban rookie, El Duque, on the mound, that is a massive deficit to overcome, and we're halfway home after a 9–3 victory.

Our confidence is so unshakeable at this point that even when former Yankee Sterling Hitchcock shuts us down in Game 3, taking a 3–0 lead into the seventh, I sit on a bullpen bench and think:

We have them just where we want them.

All season we've had different guys come through in big moments. So I am not surprised when Brosius belts a homer to lead off the seventh, or when Shane Spencer follows with a double, knocking Hitchcock out of the game. One inning later, Brosius steps in against Trevor Hoffman, one of the best closers in the business, and sends another ball over the wall, this time with two men on.

Now we're up, 5–3, and after a few hairy moments, I finish off a 5–4 victory by striking out Andy Sheets with the tying run at third. With a sweep one victory away, Andy out-pitches Brown, leaving with a 3–0 lead in the seventh with one out and two guys on. Jeff Nelson comes in and strikes out Vaughn, and then Mr. T calls for me. I run in from the pen, and am not thinking about dogpiles or trophies or anything else. I am thinking:

Get an out.

Ken Caminiti singles to load the bases, and who should come up but Jim Leyritz. He seems to be following me around. Leyritz can crush anybody's fastball if it's not well located. On a 1–2 pitch, I throw a cutter, a little up and away. Leyritz swings, but it is not the contact he is looking for and Bernie makes a basket catch in short center field.

My cousin leads off the ninth, and singles up the middle in the only at-bat he ever has against me, but he is not on first long. Carlos Hernández, the catcher, hits into a double play, and now I am looking at Mark Sweeney, a left-handed pinch hitter. I pump in two fastballs, and then come with a cutter away that he bounces to Brosius, who throws to Tino, and now the dogpile is *all* I am thinking of. Joe Girardi arrives first and hugs me as I raise my arms straight overhead, thanking the Lord. Soon I am engulfed by the World Series MVP, Scott Brosius, and everybody else. My postseason ends with six saves and 13.1 scoreless innings. It is the first time in my life I've gotten the last out of a season. It's a feeling I could get used to.

NOTES FROM MO

Just Say No to Performance-Enhancing Drugs

I have never taken steroids. I know there are people who doubt this. I heard the whispers after the dramatic increase in the speed of my fastball in 1995. I understand the distrust after so many star athletes, from Lance Armstrong to Mark McGwire, finally owned up to taking drugs after years of denying everything.

But here is the truth as it relates to me—I have never cheated, and never would.

I understand that there are players who are desperate to keep playing who feel that drugs are the only way to get the extra edge they need. But at what cost? Using PEDs is bad for our sport. It wrecks the honor of the game. Who wants to be in the record book if what you achieved has to be marked with an asterisk?

Even more than terrible sportsmanship, though, drug use is a terrible thing to do to your body. Steroids can cause acne, baldness, liver damage, and increased aggressiveness, known as 'roid rage. Boys: The person suggesting you juice up will probably not mention that steroids can cause your breasts to grow and your testicles to shrink. People who stop using PEDs can experience depression. There are even cases of suicide linked to steroid withdrawal.

Wow. Why would anybody risk their life to hit a few more home runs, or add five miles per hour to their fastball?

Enter Sandman

My worst outing as a closer comes on a hot Friday night at Yankee Stadium in July 1999. The Atlanta Braves are in town, and it is a strange game from the start. The pitching matchup is Greg Maddux vs. El Duque. Who would ever guess Maddux would give up nine hits and five runs, and El Duque would give up eight hits and six runs—and they'd both be gone before the game was half-over?

Derek, in the middle of the best year of his

life, hits his fifteenth homer and knocks three hits, raising his average to .377. Ramiro Mendoza is sensational in relief and gets us to the ninth with three-plus innings of scoreless ball. We have a 7–6 lead in the ninth when I run in from the bullpen, accompanied by the guitar riffs of Metallica's "Enter Sandman," the new entrance song the Yankees have picked for me.

I finish my warm-ups, and am standing on the back of the mound, head bowed, ball in my right hand. I'm about to say my customary prayer, asking the Lord to keep me and my teammates safe, and to give me the strength I need to do my job. Although I converted twenty of my first twenty-one save opportunities this season, I have hit a rough patch, blowing two saves in my last four chances. I have also given up four extra-base hits in those games, including two homers.

Why it comes to me when I'm standing on the mound in front of 50,000 people, I don't know, but it hits me at that moment what's wrong. I have gotten carried away with my own sense of importance. I feel utterly humbled as I come to this realization. I feel shaken to the core.

It is time to pitch now.

Oh boy, I am thinking. *I really don't know how this is going to go.*

I get Bret Boone on a fly ball to right, and for a moment I think that maybe I can steady myself after all.

The thought does not last for long.

I walk Chipper Jones, then allow a single to Brian Jordan. I fall behind Ryan Klesko, and Mel comes out to calm me down. I nod. I act as if everything is okay.

It is not okay.

Klesko laces a single. That blows the save. Two batters later, Andruw Jones takes me over the wall in left center. That blows the game.

I don't say a word about my revelation on the mound to any of my teammates—it is a personal, spiritual moment between me and God. But I have learned an important lesson. I am a human being, and human beings lose their way sometimes. I recommit myself to knowing my place in the world, to not getting too big for my pin-striped britches.

I give up one run for the rest of the year, finishing the season with streaks of thirty and two-thirds scoreless innings and twenty-two consecutive saves.

We win sixteen fewer games than we did the year before, but our record of 98–64 is still the best in the American League, putting us in the division series against the Rangers for the third time in four years. The Rangers are a very good club, but, let's face it, they tend to wilt like a flower in the Texas heat at the very sight of us. (I can only say that now that I have retired. Otherwise, a statement like that would be asking for trouble.) We sweep the series against them, and for the second straight year, they score only one run in the three games. I get the save in Game 2, and throw two more scoreless innings to finish the series and put us into the ALCS against the Red Sox—the matchup everybody seems to want.

Ever since he arrived from Cuba, Orlando "El Duque" Hernández keeps proving himself as a big-game pitcher. In Game 1, he goes eight strong innings, leaving with a 3–3 tie. I come in to start the ninth and get six outs to get us to the bottom of the tenth, when Bernie socks one over the fence a few minutes after midnight.

It's a rousing way to start, and we don't let up. Chuck Knoblauch has an RBI double and Paul O'Neill an RBI single late in Game 2, then Ramiro gets two immense outs with the bases loaded in the eighth. Then, with the tying run on third, I get the third out in the ninth for the save, and the win.

We head to Boston with a 2–0 lead. The

Red Sox get one back with a 13–1 victory—in which Pedro Martínez is brilliant and Roger Clemens, longtime Sox ace–turned–Boston's Public Enemy No. 1, has the worst postseason start of his life—but our slide stops there. Andy is dominant in Game 3. Ricky Ledee hits a grand slam in the ninth inning and we win, 9–2, dancing on the Fenway infield after El Duque lifts us to a 6–1 victory in the decisive Game 5.

That pits us against the Braves in another World Series, and wouldn't you know it, the Game 1 matchup is El Duque and Greg Maddux. I marvel at the contrast between these pitchers, and how they go about their craft. Here you have El Duque, with his spring-loaded leg kick and gyrations, and arm angles he seems to invent as he goes, throwing all kinds of nasty stuff. There you have Maddux, as steady as a metronome, commanding the ball with flawless mechanics. Unlike in the regular-season game, they are both in peak form, and we are tied 1–1 in the eighth. It stays tight until Paul O'Neill comes up that inning.

This World Series isn't especially dramatic—another four-game sweep. People remember how I break three of Ryan Klesko's bats in one at-bat and how Chipper Jones laughs about it in the dugout.

For the team, it is special because it has not been an easy year for many of us personally. Mr. T begins the season with a leave of absence to get cancer treatment. Both Scott Brosius and Luis Sojo lose their fathers. Paul's father dies in the early morning hours before Game 4. I see him at his locker before the game, and I know he is suffering but now is not the time to console him. That comes five hours later, after I break Klesko's bats and get Keith Lockhart to fly out to finish off the sweep.

As the guys all converge on me in the center of the diamond, Paulie is the last one to arrive, the joy and grief hitting him all at once. He hugs Mr. T and begins to cry. He leaves the field in tears and walks into the dugout. In the clubhouse chaos, I find Paulie at his locker.

"I am so sorry about your father," I say. "I don't know why the Lord wanted him to come home today, but I am sure he's very proud of you."

"Thank you, Mo," he says. "He was watching, guarantee you that, and he's happier than anybody that we did it."

I face forty-three batters in three postseason series that year, and none of them scores. The last run I gave up was almost three months and forty innings ago, on a double by Tampa Bay catcher John Flaherty. I finish the season with more saves (forty-five) than hits allowed (forty-three). I am named World Series MVP, and my family in Puerto Caimito tells me I am the talk of Panama.

In New York City, they throw us another

ticker-tape parade. It is easy to see how being a successful athlete can make you feel like you are something special. You ride through that canyon of skyscrapers, with millions of pieces of confetti swirling and almost as many fans cheering, and the outpouring is a humbling spectacle. All this love, all this adoration—it's remarkable to bask in so much happiness. My most enduring memory of that 1999 celebration comes at the City Hall ceremony. Mr. T has the microphone and summons Jorge Posada to join him.

"Tell them what we say at the end of our meetings, Jorgie," Mr. T says.

"Grind it out!" Jorgie hollers.

Notes from Mo

My Heavy Metal Marching Music

The opening guitar chords of Metallica's "Enter Sandman" blare over the speakers and by the time the drums kick in a few seconds later, everyone at Yankee Stadium knows what is about to happen.

It is time for me to make my run from the bullpen to the mound.

I can thank Trevor Hoffman for this. Ever since we played the San Diego Padres in the 1998 World Series and the Yankees management noticed how San Diego fans got fired up by Trevor's entrance song, "Hell's Bells" by AC/DC, they decided I needed a dramatic musical introduction, too.

For a while they try "Welcome to the Jungle," by Guns N' Roses, and then the same band's "Paradise City," but the fan reaction isn't what they want. Then one day an operations worker named Mike Luzzi decides what I need is something cool and ominous. He brings his own CD to the Stadium and cues up "Enter Sandman" by Metallica.

The fans love it. The search is over. If they had asked me, I would probably have suggested "Onward, Christian Soldiers." But I am not consulted and don't need to be. If the fans like it, let's go with it.

The Subway Series
Returns

His fierce commitment to grinding it out wins Jorgie the starting catcher's job when Joe Girardi leaves for the Chicago Cubs in 2000. Drafted as a second baseman, Jorgie spends years refining his footwork, pitch-blocking, and throwing mechanics—and now it pays off. He puts up an All-Star season, hitting twenty-eight homers with eighty-six runs batted in and the highest on-base percentage on the club. He strikes out more than anybody, too, but I cut him slack on that because he is a total gamer.

Jorgie is emotional and strong-willed, but he's a guy you want on your team, for sure. We're in St. Petersburg in July 2000 to play the Rays, and we're in a tailspin, having lost seven of the past nine games. El Duque is pitching well, but he and the Rays' batters are barking at each other. Jorge calms El Duque down—which is funny because Jorge often motivates El Duque by riling him up. In other words, the atmosphere at Tropicana Field is a bit tense.

In the bottom of the seventh, the Rays' Bobby Smith strikes out, and as Jorgie pops up to return the ball, Smith bumps him slightly. Jorgie takes offense and jabs the ball into Smith's side and they're off, bodies tumbling. Both are ejected (and later suspended), and even though I never ask Jorgie why he got into it with Smith, he knows how to rouse the troops. Getting out of our slump means so much that Mr. T has me come in to close even though we have a five-run lead. We win seven of our next eight and climb back into first place—for the rest of the year.

When you go through such long seasons, ups and downs are inevitable, both for the team and for individual players. In 2000, more than anybody else on the team I feel for Chuck Knoblauch, who was a huge part of our championship runs in 1998 and 1999. For almost a decade he's been one of the top lead-off men in baseball. He also won a Gold Glove as the league's top defensive second baseman, which is why it's so hard to see him with the "yips," the term baseball people use for players who suddenly, inexplicably, lose the ability to execute a basic skill. It can be a pitcher who loses the strike zone and never relocates it, a catcher who can't throw the ball back to the pitcher, or, in Chuck's case, a second baseman who can't make a twenty-five-foot throw to the first baseman right next door. Chuck is fine when he has to make a diving play, then scramble to his feet and throw. The yips come when he has time to think about it. I've never been on a team with a player who has had the yips until now, and it's just horrific to watch. Chuck toughs it out, and gets better toward the end of the year, but by then our issues go way beyond the yips. When Roger defeats the Blue Jays and I get my thirty-fourth save on September 13, we are twenty-five games over .500, at which point we sink faster than my father's rusty old anchor.

We lose fifteen of our last eighteen games. In our last seven games—all losses—we are outscored, 68–15. That's hard for an expansion team to do, never mind the defending World Series champion.

So we limp into the division series against the Oakland A's, and when Roger gives up four runs in six innings to lose Game 1 we are up against it in a way we haven't been since 1997. Could it be that the Mets, who are on their way to winning the National League pennant, are the team that will get the ticker-tape parade this fall?

Not many managers have better instincts than Mr. T, so when he changes the lineup for Game 2, I don't think of it as panic; it's a smart manager playing a hunch. Knoblauch, now a designated hitter because of his throwing issues, sits down; Glenallen Hill takes over. Paulie, struggling with a bad hip, moves down in the order, and Jorge moves up to the second spot, right behind Derek. Hill and Luis Sojo deliver big hits, and Jorgie is on base three times. Andy pitches brilliantly, taking a shutout through seven and two-thirds, and then Mr. T calls for me. I get four groundouts to complete a 4–0 victory, even the series, and remind us what it feels like to win.

Back at Yankee Stadium, El Duque outduels Tim Hudson, and I get the last six outs without giving up a hit. The 4–2 victory puts us a game away from the ALCS but Roger gets spanked around again and the A's go on to an 11–1 rout. So it's back to Oakland, where we post six runs in the first and give five of them back before I finally get the save at 7–5 to put us up against Piniella and his Mariners in the ALCS.

No one said it would be easy, right?

The ALCS against the Mariners produces one of the truly great pitching performances that I have ever seen, delivered by Roger in Game 4, who allows one hit while striking out fifteen. Clemens's heroics give us a three-games-to-one lead. In Game 6, David Justice, the series MVP, rips a massive homer to power a six-run seventh that gives us a 9–4 lead. It's 9–5 when I come on to close in the eighth, and I give up two more runs to make it 9–7. In the ninth, I get two outs on five pitches before Alex Rodriguez gets on with an infield hit. This isn't good.

Because the next hitter is the Mo-killer, Edgar Martínez.

I fire strike one, and then come at him again, trying to stay in so he can't smack the ball the other way, something he is very good at. The cutter breaks hard and late. Edgar swings but hits it weakly, a grounder to short. Derek scoops it up and throws over to Tino.

What do you know?

I actually got Edgar Martínez out.

An instant later, Jorge is rushing to hug me, and Derek races in and rams me with a body check.

"Edgar Martínez can't hit you," Derek says.

The crowd chants, "We want the Mets." They will get the Mets, and so will we—the first Subway Series since 1956.

The intensity of the rivalry between the Yankees, the Mets, and their fans is still new to me. It's not as if half the fishermen on our boat are wearing Mets jerseys and the other half, Yankees caps. We don't spend our days debating who is better, Keith Hernandez or Don Mattingly.

But it doesn't take long to realize this is going to be a very different World Series from the previous three. Nothing changes with the goal: Win four games. I'm not going to get caught up in the hysteria and Super Bowl–style craziness. But to be in a Series that requires no flights (a good thing), and lets me sleep in my own bed and wake up with my family every day (an even better thing), and that is being covered by about ten million reporters, well, it's not the same. The spotlight feels bigger, and brighter.

Despite our dismal playing down the stretch, we are back to our winning baseball ways. All credit must go to Mr. T and his staff for that. They have created a culture of deep belief in ourselves, without arrogance. That is such a fine line you can't even see it, but we walk it. You know how many times I've gone out to the mound thinking, *This guy has no shot, because I am Mariano Rivera*?

Never.

The guy with the bat is a professional. He is a big league hitter, whether his name is Mike Piazza or Bubba Trammell or Benny Agbayani. He wants a hit as bad as I want an out. I respect every competitor, from Edgar Martínez to the guy who has never hit a fair ball off of me.

The Series begins at Yankee Stadium, with the Mets sending out someone else I respect—Al Leiter. He is already a world champion, having pitched six gritty innings in Game 7 with the 1997 Marlins. Leiter and Andy match zeroes through five innings, and then Timo Pérez, a fleet outfielder whose energy and pop have been a big piece of the Mets' run late in the year, singles up the middle.

I am still in the clubhouse when, with two outs, Todd Zeile crushes a line drive to left. It looks as if it's going out, but the ball hits the top of the wall, and plops onto the warning track. David Justice, our left fielder, picks it up and hits the cutoff man, Derek, who takes the throw, spins, and fires a strike to Jorge, who blocks the plate to prevent Pérez from scoring.

It's just a perfect throw by Derek, all the more so because he is off balance. It is a terrible play by Pérez, who is so sure the ball is gone that he is running half speed as he rounds second. If he's running even three-quarter speed, he scores standing up.

In the bottom of the inning, Justice hits a two-run double and we have just nine outs to get, but the Mets come back, taking a 3–2 lead on a two-run single by pinch hitter Trammell and, with Jeff Nelson on in relief, a well-placed roller down the third-base line by Edgardo Alfonzo.

Out in the pen now, I wait for the phone to ring.

It rings a moment later. Tony Cloninger, the bullpen coach, answers.

"Mo," Tony says.

That is all I need to hear. I warm up with a weighted three-pound ball, windmilling my arm around as I bend at the waist. Then I follow my usual routine with Borzi: three easy tosses as he stands behind the plate, then half dozen or so pitches to his glove side, another half dozen to the other side, then come back to the glove side. In fifteen to eighteen pitches, I am loose.

I enter in the top of the ninth. Jay Payton, leading off, flies out. I nick Todd Pratt with a pitch, give up a double to Kurt Abbott, and have myself a mess. Pérez steps up. I need a strikeout or a ground ball right to somebody, with the infield in. On a 1–2 pitch, I come inside hard with the cutter and Pérez taps it to second for the second out. I get Alfonzo, a very tough hitter, swinging.

Now, it's our last chance to tie or win the game against the Mets closer, Armando Benítez. Jorge fights off seven pitches before hitting a long fly out. Paulie steps in and tries to change recent history. He is thirty-seven years old, has a bad hip, and has been slumping, but if there's one guy who is going to battle to the end, it's Paulie. Benítez jumps ahead, 1–2. A massive man with an intimidating fastball, Benítez keeps pumping in high-nineties heaters, and Paulie keeps fouling them off. With two strikes, Benítez misses twice to run the count to 3–2. Now the pressure is even. Paulie spoils another strike, and another, and the crowd is starting to roar. Benítez is getting exasperated.

On the tenth pitch of the at-bat, Benítez misses outside and Paulie takes his hard-won walk. It's as good an at-bat as I've ever seen. The Stadium is rocking. Pinch-hitting for Brosius, Luis Polonia hits a single to right, and José Vizcaíno goes the other way, knocking a single to left that's too shallow for Paulie to score. Knoblauch hits a sacrifice fly that sends O'Neill home to tie the game at three-all.

I strike out Piazza and Zeile and get Robin Ventura to fly out to take care of the tenth, and then Mike Stanton throws two strong innings and Game 1 moves to the bottom of the twelfth. It's approaching one in the morning. We've been playing baseball for four and a half hours.

This is just the kind of game we find a way to grind out and win, I think.

I pick my moments to be vocal in the dugout. I usually only do it in the most important games. Games like this one.

"Now is the time," I say, walking up and down the dugout. "Let's win this right now."

With one out, Tino singles and Jorge doubles off Mets reliever Turk Wendell. The Mets walk Paulie to load the bases and force an out at the plate. Luis Sojo pops up, and now it's Vizcaíno's turn. He already has two hits, another of Mr. T's hunches that works brilliantly. On Wendell's first pitch, Vizcaíno swings and serves a line drive into left. Here comes Tino, and there goes Vizcaíno, leaping his way around first. It is 1:04 on a Sunday morning. We pour onto the field and mob Viz. It's a game that we win on a relay throw, a ten-pitch walk, and three hits from a Dominican journeyman on his seventh team.

He fits right in. He knows how to win.

Nineteen hours after Viz's game-winner, I am in a hot tub in the trainer's room. There is no TV in there, but I know the Mets' All-Star catcher, Mike Piazza, is the third man up against Roger. If you believe the media, it is the most anticipated heavyweight showdown since Muhammad Ali and Joe Frazier. I don't buy into the hype, but I *am* curious to see what happens.

When we played the Mets in early June, Piazza hit a grand slam against Clemens.

When we played the Mets in early July, Clemens hit Piazza in the head with a fastball.

I can't say what Clemens's intentions are; I never talk to him about it. And pitchers have the right to back a batter off the plate with something inside. But you never do something that endangers somebody's livelihood or even their life. Good ol' country hardball? To me, it's more like good ol' country cowardice, throwing a baseball at somebody's head. This man with the bat is somebody's son. He is probably somebody's husband and somebody's father. You can't ignore that. I compete as hard as anybody, but it must be done within the confines of fair play. Headhunting is not fair play.

By the time I get to a TV, I have missed all the excitement, so I immediately catch a replay: Clemens has two strikes on Piazza when he comes inside with a fastball. Piazza swings, breaking his bat, the barrel bouncing right toward the mound. Unaware the ball is foul, he runs toward first. Clemens picks up the bat barrel and flings it sidearm, and hard, toward Piazza as he's running up the first-base line. The bat skims along the ground and kicks up, its jagged edge missing Piazza by a foot.

"What's your problem?" Piazza says, taking a step toward the mound. The umpire quickly steps between Roger and Piazza. The benches empty in a New York minute but calm is restored before the situation deteriorates any further. I have no idea why Roger would do that, but it's mind-boggling to me that you could be so emotionally wound up that you snap that way. Roger is an insanely intense competitor.

Piazza grounds out on the next pitch for a 1-2-3 inning.

Mike Hampton, the Mets starter, is wild early, helping us score two in the first. Brosius leads off the second with a shot into the seats and we've tacked on three more when I run into George Steinbrenner in the clubhouse. I'm thirty years old, but he still calls me "Kid."

I call him "Mr. George."

"Kid, you want a hot dog? I'll get you a hot dog."

"No thanks, Mr. George. I'm good."

"Hey, Kid, we going to win this Series? What do you think?"

"We are going to win, and I am so sure I will make you a bet, Mr. George. If I am right and we win, you'll fly my wife and kids and me to Panama on your private jet. If I am wrong, I will take you out to dinner at the restaurant of your choice."

"You got a bet, Kid," Mr. George says.

Mr. George disappears and I head for the bullpen. Roger pitches eight shutout innings and passes the ball to Jeff Nelson in the ninth with a 6–0 lead. The game seems about as safe as it can be, until it isn't. Piazza hits a two-run homer. Robin Ventura singles. With no one out, I replace Nelson, but the key substitution is Clay Bellinger, slotted into left for defense. He saves my tail by making a superb catch at the fence of a Todd Zeile drive. Agbayani singles, but then I get Lenny Harris on a fielder's choice. I have two outs and two guys on, when Payton, the Mets center fielder, hits an outside cutter into the seats in right.

Suddenly, the score is 6–5. The growing panic in the Stadium is palpable. Kurt Abbott steps up. He doubled off me in Game 1. Here's what I am thinking:

This game needs to end now.

I like tidy 1-2-3 innings, and this has turned into a fiasco. I get ahead, 0–2, on Abbott, and fire the next cutter just where I want it, high on the inner half. Abbott takes, and the home plate umpire rings him up. Abbott has a brief fit as Jorge comes out to shake my hand. Fifty-six thousand fans can breathe again.

I face 309 more hitters in my postseason career. Jay Payton is the last one to hit a home run off me.

After a travel day—to give us time to get the 9.5 miles from Yankee Stadium to Queens—the Mets, losers of two agonizing one-run games, return home to Shea Stadium. I'm surprised at how many Yankee fans have found their way into enemy territory, but it doesn't stop the Mets from knocking El Duque around in Game 3 and taking a 4–2 victory behind Rick Reed.

We're not getting a lot of production from our leadoff guys—they are 0 for 12 in the three games—so Mr. T moves Derek to the top spot for Game 4. Bobby Jones is the Mets starter, and Derek drives his first pitch of the game over the left-center-field wall at Shea Stadium. It's a single run that feels like ten, for the way it fires us up and stuns the home team. Jones gives up two more runs before steadying himself. Meanwhile, Piazza hits another two-run homer to pull the Mets within a run. When he comes up again in the fifth with two out and nobody on, Mr. T wants a fresh arm, and calls for David Cone from the pen. David is thirty-seven, an ace-turned-forgotten man, coming off the worst season of his tremendous career, a yearlong struggle that ended with a 4–14 record and

6.91 ERA. He hasn't thrown a single pitch in this World Series.

It's another Mr. T hunch, that David can find a way to get Piazza. David gets ahead, 1–2, and comes right at Piazza with a sharp slider. Piazza pops it up for the third out.

Both bullpens pitch flawlessly and now it's on me in the eighth and ninth. Paulie makes a fine grab of a sinking liner by Alfonzo to lead off the eighth, and then I get Piazza to ground out, before Zeile singles. I get out of it by popping up Ventura, and record two quick outs in the ninth, too.

Next up is Matt Franco, who had a game-winning hit against me the year before. On the first pitch, a strike, Jorge and I can tell Franco is waiting for the cutter in on the hands, edging farther from the plate to give him more room to turn on it.

Jorge catches my attention and points to his eyes, as if to say:

You see that?

I do see it. I nod. I buzz a fastball on the

outside corner, and Franco never moves. Strike two. I know he's sitting on the cutter in. Jorge knows it, too. I buzz another fastball on the outside corner. Franco never moves again.

Game over.

In four games, we have fifteen runs, and the Mets have fourteen. Every game pivots on one or two plays, or one or two pitches. I like the way the pivots have been going, and now it's time to finish things up in Game 5, Leiter vs. Andy, a rematch of Game 1.

Bernie, in an 0-for-16 slump in the Series, rips a homer to start the second, and after the Mets answer with two runs in the bottom of the inning, Derek takes two tight fastballs from Leiter and then pounds his second homer in two games. It's 2–2, and Andy and Leiter are pitching their left arms off, matching zeroes and guts. Mike Stanton comes on for a 1-2-3 eighth, and Leiter comes back out for the ninth and gets two quick strikeouts.

With Leiter nearing one hundred forty

pitches, Jorge, the guy with the best eye on the team, keeps fighting off pitches, battling the way Paulie did in the ninth inning of Game 1. After a nine-pitch drama, Jorge walks. Scott Brosius drills a single to left. Luis Sojo swings at the first pitch and hits a ten-hop single through the middle. Jorgie is running on the first bounce so he can score from second. Payton tries to throw him out at the plate, but the ball hits Jorgie and careens into the dugout, allowing Scott to score, too. We're up 4–2 now, three outs away. As I warm up, I think about making the first pitch I throw as good as it can be.

The pinch hitter is Darryl Hamilton. He strikes out on three pitches.

Next up is Agbayani, the left fielder. I walk him on four straight. Bad thing to do, putting the tying run at the plate, but it's done. I let it go. I shift my focus to Alfonzo, get ahead, 1–2, and fire a cutter away. He lofts a ball to right that Paulie catches.

It is now down to Mike Piazza, one of the

most dangerous hitters in baseball. Derek and Sojo trot to the mound for a visit. Derek does the talking.

"You want to be careful here. You know what he can do. Move the ball around and go after him hard," Derek says.

He slaps me on the leg with his glove and returns to short. I blow on my right hand. I look in at Jorge's glove. I am not overthinking this. I am going to throw the best pitch I can.

I am going to keep it simple.

Piazza has tremendous opposite-field power. I want to stay in on him. My first pitch is a cutter, in. Strike one. Jorge sets up inside again, calling for the ball a little higher. I deliver a cutter not quite as in as I want, a few inches out over the plate. Piazza takes a rip and hits the ball pretty well, a fly to center. I turn and watch Bernie's body language as he is easing back, completely in control. A few steps in front of the track, he makes the catch, and at exactly midnight on October 27, 2000, Bernie goes down on a knee, bowing his head in momentary prayer. Now both my arms are in the air and I am jumping up and down, up and down, until Tino arrives for a hug, the whole team pours onto the field, and the tension and stress of big-time competition evaporate faster than a puddle in the Panamanian sun.

The day after we win, I get a phone call from Mr. George's assistant.

"Good morning," she says. "Mr. Steinbrenner asked me to call. Are you ready to make the arrangements for your trip to Panama?"

NOTES FROM MO

"A Synonym for Civil War"

There are a few other American cities with subway systems, but only New York can boast about playing host to a Subway Series—a matchup between teams that call the same city home and whose fans can share public transportation to and from the games.

The New York City subway opened in 1904, connecting Manhattan with three of the city's four "outer boroughs"—Queens, Brooklyn, and the Bronx, where the Yankees have played since 1923. (To get to the fifth borough, you can ride the Staten Island Ferry for free! But there's only minor league baseball there.)

At the time, New York had three major league baseball teams: the Yankees, the New York Giants, and the Brooklyn Dodgers, who played at Ebbets Field. (The name "Dodgers" arose from fans "dodging" the turnstiles at the entrance to, first, the public trolleys and, later, the subway, to avoid paying the nickel fare.)

The Yankees lost the first two Subway Series to the Giants, in 1921 and 1922, then turned the table on their former stadium-mates, beating the Giants in 1923, 1936, and 1937.

But the rivalry that turned the Subway Series into what one baseball writer called "a synonym for Civil War" was between the Yankees and the Dodgers, who met in the World Series *seven times* between 1941 and 1956. The Yankees won six of the seven meetings. The Dodgers were World Champions only once, in 1955.

The concept of a Subway Series nearly disappeared in 1958, when both the Giants and the Dodgers moved their teams to California. New York baseball fans were left with only the Yankees to root for until the establishment of the New York Metropolitans, an expansion team that played its first season in 1962. With the introduction of interleague play in 1997, now fans can look forward to at least two Subway Series a year, during the regular season.

A New Reason to Win

It's the bottom of the eighth in Baltimore and Cal Ripken, baseball's "Iron Man," is at the plate. We are a month into the 2001 season. It's a hot night, my favorite weather to pitch in. Cal's Orioles are down, 7–5, but I am ahead in the count. I check the runner at second, and deliver a hard cutter. Cal, in the last season of a legendary career, thinks it might hit him, or at least graze his No. 8 uniform. He leans back to get out of the way, just as the pitch makes a left turn, veering sharply inside.

The home plate umpire yanks up his right arm. Cal walks away, shaking his head. I walk off the Camden Yards mound, knowing it's one of those nights when my cutter is breaking like a Wiffle ball.

"You got no chance when it moves that much," Derek tells a reporter later.

We spend most of the season dominating the American League East, and when we take three straight against the Red Sox at Yankee Stadium in early September, they fall to thirteen games back. The series is scheduled to conclude on a Monday night, with Roger Clemens trying to extend his record to 20–1 against his old team. A drenching rain makes the field unplayable and the game is rained out.

The date is September 10.

By morning the rain has gone, leaving behind a hint of autumn chill and a spectacularly blue sky. It's a school day, so I am up early with the boys. I am brushing my teeth when my mother-in-law, who is staying with us, calls out. She sounds alarmed.

"Clara! Pili! Come quick! Look at what's on TV!"

I hustle to the kitchen and hear a bizarre report about a plane flying into the World Trade Center. It's not yet 9:00 a.m. One of the towers is on fire, smoke billowing out of the top. How could this have happened? I worry about the workers in the building. Will they be able to get out?

Then a second plane hits the other tower. Now things become much clearer.

This is a terrorist attack.

More tragic reports follow, about the plane that hit the Pentagon and Flight 93 crashing in the Pennsylvania countryside. The images are too horrific to comprehend, the evil behind the attack even more so. I pray for the victims and their families. I pray for all of us, for the country. The city grieves and we grieve along with it. All ball games are canceled for a week.

We pick up the season on September 18 in Comiskey Park, winning, 11–3, then return for our first game in New York since the attacks. Roger visits a New York firehouse in the afternoon before his start. It's a powerful night of tribute to the victims and the first responders. It feels more like a church service than a baseball game. Tampa beats us, 4–0, but with the Red Sox loss we clinch the AL East title for the fifth time in six years. Our celebration is very subdued. We are the New York Yankees. Our city is hurting in a big way, and so are we. It is not the time to throw a party.

Even though we win ninety-five games in 2001, we aren't close to being the premier team in the American League. With a 116–46 record, the Seattle Mariners are even better than we were in 1998, a feat so ridiculous that the Oakland A's win 102 games—and finish fourteen games out of first.

We might be three-time defending World Series champions, but we are only the third-best team in our league. We draw Oakland in the division series. In Game 1, at Yankee Stadium, Mark Mulder outpitches Roger, and the A's get three homers to win 5–3. Tim Hudson shuts us down in Game 2 and the A's go up 2–0 in the series. Now we fly west, our season riding on the right arm of Mike Mussina. The A's have won seventeen straight games at home. Barry Zito, a twenty-two-year-old left-hander, is aiming to make it eighteen. The game is scoreless through four. With one out in the fifth, Jorge drives a pitch over the wall to give us a 1–0 lead. Mussina sets the A's down in order in the sixth. He gets two quick outs, retiring Jermaine Dye and Eric Chavez in the seventh, before Jeremy Giambi singles and Terrence Long drills a 2–2 pitch inside the first-base line, past a diving Tino, and into the right-field corner. Shane Spencer retrieves it and comes up throwing, but misses both cutoff men. It is all happening right before my eyes, since the visiting bullpen is wedged along the first-base line. Giambi rounds third and will score easily to tie the game. Spencer's throw bounds toward home, along the first-base line, into no-man's-land.

That's when I see Derek running across the infield, toward the first-base line.

Where is he going? I think. *This play has nothing to do with him.*

He is in a full sprint, closing in on the ball.

Now I know what he's doing.

He is almost at the line, fifteen to twenty feet from home plate. He scoops up the rolling ball. He shovels it backhand toward Jorge.

Giambi is coming in. Standing up. Big mistake.

Jorge gets the flip and swipes a tag on Giambi, an instant before he touches home.

Giambi is out. Our 1–0 lead is intact. Derek pumps his fist. Mussina pumps his fist. I feel like running out of the bullpen and pumping my fist. Half the dugout is charging onto

I am all legs, and full of pride, the day I graduate from Victoriana Chacón Elementary School—and shake hands with Puerto Caimito mayor Eugenio Castañón.

Here I am at eighteen—right before I gave up the sport of soccer due to a serious eye injury.

Clara and me on our wedding day, November 9, 1991. Marrying her was the best decision I've ever made.

Clara and I are off to Panama City for a two-day honeymoon before I have to leave to play instructional league ball.

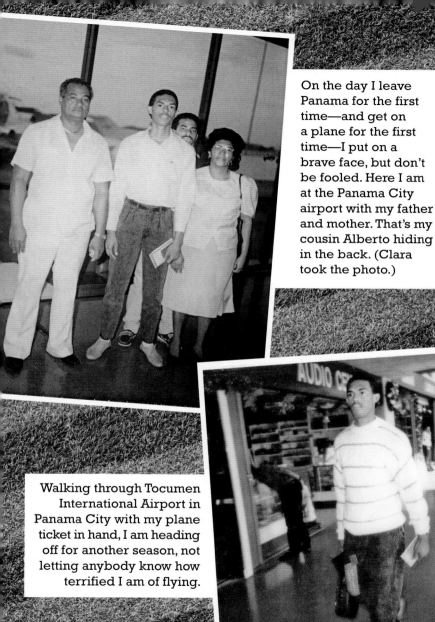

On the day I leave Panama for the first time—and get on a plane for the first time—I put on a brave face, but don't be fooled. Here I am at the Panama City airport with my father and mother. That's my cousin Alberto hiding in the back. (Clara took the photo.)

Walking through Tocumen International Airport in Panama City with my plane ticket in hand, I am heading off for another season, not letting anybody know how terrified I am of flying.

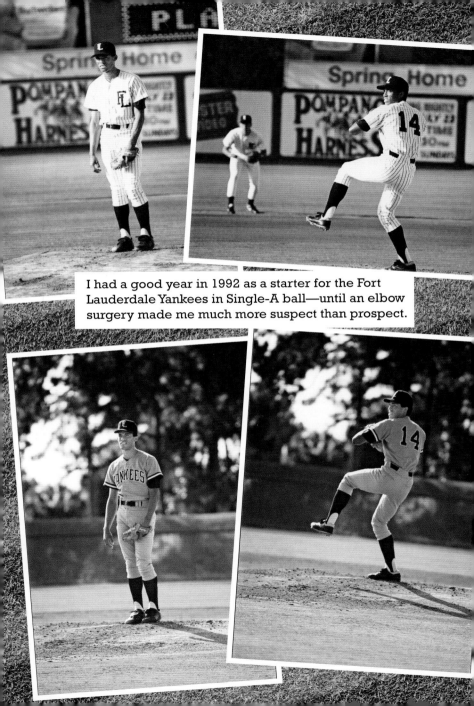

I had a good year in 1992 as a starter for the Fort Lauderdale Yankees in Single-A ball—until an elbow surgery made me much more suspect than prospect.

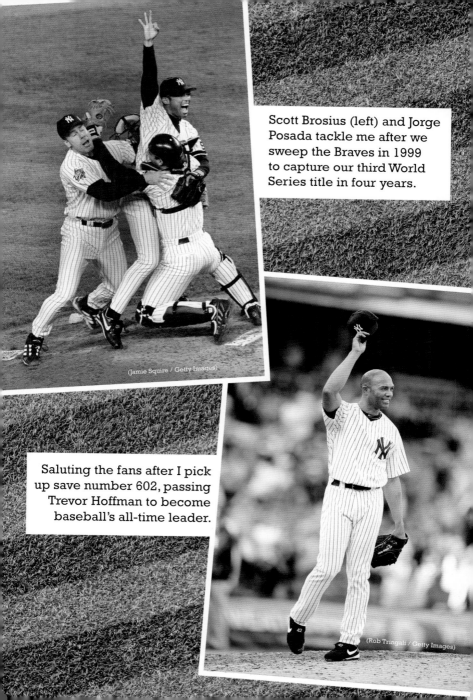

Scott Brosius (left) and Jorge Posada tackle me after we sweep the Braves in 1999 to capture our third World Series title in four years.

(Jamie Squire / Getty Images)

Saluting the fans after I pick up save number 602, passing Trevor Hoffman to become baseball's all-time leader.

(Rob Tringali / Getty Images)

Another cutter is about to be launched.

(Ronald C. Modra / Sports Imagery / Getty Images)

The last out is always the hardest one to get. Here I celebrate getting Mark Sweeney and completing our sweep of the Padres in 1998.

(Vincent Laforet / Getty Images)

Winning never gets old.

(Pool / Getty Images)

(Jim McIsaac / Getty Images)

Having consistent, repeatable mechanics is a tremendous asset for a pitcher. Here I repeat mine in one of the last pitches of my career.

About one second after my old friends Andy Pettitte and Derek Jeter came to get me with two outs in the ninth of my final game, I was sobbing in Andy's arms. I had held in my emotions for a long, long time. I was ready to let them go.

Walking off the mound for the final time on September 26, 2013—with the fans standing and cheering and the Tampa Bay Rays (background) and the Yankees both standing, too—was one of the most powerful and emotional moments of my life.

the field, a spontaneous burst of emotion for a player who never stops hustling.

It is the greatest instinctive play I have ever seen.

With six outs to go, I come on in the eighth and get three. Then I have to face the heart of the order in the ninth, starting with Jason Giambi, reigning American League MVP, and Jeremy's big—and I mean big—brother. Giambi hits a grounder to second for the first out but I give up a double to Jermaine Dye, before striking out Eric Chavez. Two out and who steps up but Giambi the Younger, the base runner who doesn't slide. For sure, he is seeking redemption but I get him to ground out, and we are still alive.

In Game 4, we get heroic pitching and hitting from El Duque and Bernie, who has three hits and five RBIs, and after a 9–2 victory, we fly three thousand miles back to New York to play Game 5 the next day. Before a single pitch is thrown, I'm struck by how different the city feels than it did before September 11. Everything feels more vivid, more urgent, somehow. It's hard to describe.

There's always energy pulsing through Yankee Stadium, but now it seems packed with more meaning, as if our mission is not only to win one more World Series, but to do it for the city.

Neither Roger nor Mark Mulder has his best stuff, but we manage a 5–3 lead through six innings. After Ramiro hurls a 1-2-3 seventh it's on me to get the last six outs. Jason Giambi singles to start the eighth, but I get Eric Chavez on a fielder's choice, bringing up Terrence Long, who pops up a pitch toward the seats behind third. Here comes Derek again, racing behind the bag and leaning over the railing to make a phenomenal catch even as he goes head over heels into the seats. Somehow he holds on to the ball for the second out, and I get Ron Gant on a groundout to finish the eighth.

In the ninth, I have two outs when pinch hitter Eric Byrnes works me to a 2–2 count. Jorge sets up inside. I fire a fastball and Byrnes swings through it, and I jump up and do a complete 360, propelled by the emotion not just of the moment, but of the whole past month. I don't remember ever spinning like that before, and I never do it again. Jorge runs out, wrapping an arm around me. Mr. T escorts New York mayor Rudolph Giuliani, who has done so much to help the city after the attacks, onto the field. It's a night supersaturated with feeling: We've come back to win three straight against a great team, embodying the city's resilient spirit.

Now, on to face the mighty Mariners.

The first two games are in Seattle. We know how good the Mariners are, and we respect what they have done this season, but we are confident we can get by them.

Andy is our Game 1 guy, and he answers another big-game start with another big-time effort, giving up only one run and striking out seven. Knoblauch's single scores Jorge in the second, and then Jorge pounds a ball from Mariners starter Aaron Sele off the wall in right in the top of the fourth, hustling all the way and daring Ichiro Suzuki to try to throw him out at second. Ichiro's throw is outstanding, but Jorge gets under the tag. Paulie drills a two-run homer to give Andy a 3–1 lead through eighth.

In the ninth, Alfonso Soriano drives a ball off reliever José Paniagua and stands at the plate to admire his hit. The ball hits the wall, and Sori winds up at first. Mr. T is furious. Sori is a gifted young hitter, but admiring home runs, rather than running, is not how we do things. As if to atone for his lapse, he steals second and then scores on a David Justice single, pushing the lead to 4–1.

I come on for the ninth, and with one out, Ichiro, a guy who handles the bat as if it is a magic wand, drops a double down the left-field line. He isn't just the league batting champion with a .350 average and 242 hits: He's on his way to being the American League MVP. I am an out away from the save when Stan Javier hits a comebacker to the mound. I get the out but twist my ankle, which had already been bothering me. The next batter is Bret Boone, and I am determined to get him out, because guess who is in the on-deck circle?

Edgar Martínez. The Mo-killer. With a better than .500 lifetime batting average against me, the odds are in his favor this time.

Instead, the first pitch I throw to Boone is wild, allowing Ichiro to go to third. My third pitch is also wild, and Ichiro scores.

I do not throw another wild pitch in the postseason for the rest of my career, but that does me no good now. Boone walks. It's obvious my mechanics are off. I have walked just four batters since the All-Star break, and now I get to face Edgar as the potential tying run.

I get strike one, and then throw a cutter away. Edgar grounds it to first. Tino digs it out and tosses it to me, covering at first for the third out.

Game 1 is ours.

Phew.

Mussina, who was so sensational in the flip-play game against Oakland, isn't quite as sharp in Game 2 but gets an early 3–0 lead thanks to a Brosius two-run double. Unfortunately, the Mariners are doing what our hitters usually do: They are making Moose work. In the bottom of the second, Javier works a nine-pitch at-bat for a walk; Dan Wilson fouls off seven straight pitches then singles. Moose gets out of it, but Javier hits a two-run homer in the fourth and now it's a one-run game. Moose grinds through six, keeping it close. There's nothing better than seeing a guy compete so hard and get good results on a day when he doesn't have his best stuff.

Ramiro takes over in the seventh, and with one on and two out, Mr. T makes a brave call, ordering Ramiro to walk Ichiro. You are not supposed to put the potential winning run on base—ever—but Ichiro is just too dangerous to worry about what the book says. Mark McLemore taps out to second, so Mr. T looks like the strategic genius he is once again.

I enter with one out in the eighth and my good pal Edgar on first. (At least he got his single off Ramiro, though at the time, that is cold comfort.) I erase him when Olerud hits into a force-out.

Cameron strikes out to end the eighth and so does David Bell to end the game.

We're up 2–0 and head back east, halfway to the World Series.

El Duque doesn't have it and the bullpen gets rocked in Game 3. The Mariners win, 14–3. The visiting team has now won all three games. If we can stop the trend, we can avoid a return trip to Safeco Field. We've got Roger, who struck out fifteen Mariners the last time they saw him in the playoffs, and they've got Paul Abbott, who won seventeen games during the season but had a disastrous start against the Indians in the division series. He occasionally has what we call "control issues."

This is one of those occasions. Abbott walks eight guys in five innings, throwing forty-nine strikes and forty-eight balls. Somehow he manages to get an out when he really needs one, however; he's no-hit us through five innings.

Limited by a bad hamstring, Roger goes five, giving up only one hit. The bullpens take over. In the eighth, we're still scoreless. Ramiro gets the first two outs, about to finish three innings of no-hit ball, when Bret Boone pelts a changeup into the seats. The Mariners have a 1–0 lead—and are six outs away from tying the series at two-all.

Arthur Rhodes comes out of the Mariners' pen in the bottom of the inning. He is a leftie who, for whatever reason, is good against the rest of the league but not very good against us. With one out and a full count to Bernie, Rhodes throws a fastball, his best pitch, out over the plate. Bernie hits a high fly that drops into the seats, just beyond the glove of a leaping Ichiro. The game is tied. The next pitcher to enter the game is me, not for a save. Just to keep it tied.

Olerud grounds out on my first pitch. Javier pushes a bunt toward second and is out on my second pitch. Cameron pops out on my third pitch. I am on the mound for about ninety seconds, maybe less. I am surprised that Cameron doesn't take a pitch or two, because one of baseball's unwritten rules is: Don't let the opposing pitcher have a three-pitch inning.

Not that I am complaining.

Kazuhiro Sasaki, the Mariners' closer, comes on for the ninth and gets Shane Spencer on a groundout. Then Brosius smacks a ball up the middle that McLemore stops, but can't relay to first in time to beat Brosius there. Up steps Soriano. Sasaki throws a splitter, low. Soriano is a free swinger, but doesn't offer. Sasaki doesn't want to get behind in the count but doesn't want to push the winning run into scoring position, either. So he throws a fastball, waist-high, directly over the middle of the plate. Soriano drives it to far right center. Mike Cameron climbs the wall but has no shot. Our star rookie, who breaks into the big leagues with eighteen homers and seventy-three RBIs, has put us a game away from the World Series. The fans go berserk. It seems to get louder every time somebody produces another round of late-inning heroics.

Game 5 is the next day, and our philosophy is: Why wait? You don't want to give a club that won 116 games reason to hope. Aaron Sele, another pitcher who pitches better against anybody but the Yankees, throws two scoreless innings before we break out, scoring four times in the third, the big hit a two-run homer by Bernie. Paulie homers off Sele an inning later, and with Andy cruising, we feel safe, especially after we pile on four more runs against the Mariners bullpen. The crowd starts chanting, "Overrated," at the Mariners and, "No Game Six," at their manager, Lou Piniella, who had guaranteed that the series would return to Seattle. I don't like this kind of taunting and never have. I don't like the idea of mocking anybody. But at the moment, I am focused on getting back to the World Series to bring home a fourth straight title.

Mr. T brings me in to close with a nine-run lead, 12–3. On my twelfth pitch, Mike Cameron hits a soft liner, and Spencer, who comes on for defense in the late innings, runs it down. The whole team mobs the mound, pinstripes everywhere, all of us taking turns hugging each other. In consecutive series, we've beaten the two best teams in the game this season.

There are four more games to win.

The Series opens in Phoenix, in a ballpark with a swimming pool in center field. We don't go for a dip, but we might as well because nobody is hitting except for Bernie, who has an RBI double off of Curt Schilling in the first.

After Bernie's hit, however, our bats go utterly silent. Brosius doubles in the second and Jorge singles in the fourth, and that is the sum total of Yankee offense. Schilling goes seven innings, strikes out eight, and wins his fourth game against no losses in the postseason. Mussina, who has been our surest hand the last month, gets taken deep by Craig Counsell and Luis Gonzalez. We lose 9–1.

Then it's Johnson against Andy in Game 2, and the news gets worse: Johnson is even more dominant than Schilling was. He gives up no runs and three hits, while recording eleven strikeouts in a complete-game master-piece. Matt Williams socks a three-run homer off Andy and the Diamondbacks win 4–0. It might as well be 40–0 for the way Johnson is pitching.

We fly back to New York, putting our season in Roger's hands. Jorge gives us an early lead with a homer off Brian Anderson, the Diamondbacks starter. Roger dodges a bases-loaded jam early and escapes again in the sixth when Shane Spencer makes a sprawling catch of a searing Matt Williams liner that saves two runs. Brosius hits a single to give us a 2–1 lead in the sixth and Roger finishes strong, with two punch-outs in the seventh in a 1-2-3 inning. Then he gives the ball to me.

I haven't pitched in eight days, but I feel sharp. I get Counsell, bunting for a base hit, then strike out Steve Finley and Gonzalez. I get two more Ks in the ninth, before Williams bounces out to end it. It's a huge win for us, with Schilling set to go again in Game 4.

Schilling is just as good as he was in Game 1, but El Duque matches him. Tied at one, the game goes into the eighth, Mike Stanton on the mound. Gonzalez singles, and Erubiel Durazo, the DH, pounds a double, and the Diamondbacks go up, 3–1. Their closer, the South Korean submariner Byung-Hyun Kim, has been untouchable in the playoffs, with his heavy sinker and nasty delivery. He goes to full counts on Spencer, Brosius, and Sori in the bottom of the eighth. He strikes out all three.

Ramiro plows through a clean ninth, and now we're down to our last three outs. Derek tries to bunt his way on; Williams, the third baseman, throws him out. After Paulie singles to left, Bernie goes down swinging on three pitches and now it's on Tino. We are one out from being down three games to one, with Randy Johnson next, and probably Schilling again if it comes to that. We have a pulse, but it's faint. Kim checks Paulie and delivers, belt-high to the outside part of the plate. If Tino tries to pull it, it's a ground ball to second, or maybe a weak pop-up to center.

But Tino doesn't try to pull it. He brings the barrel around and mashes the pitch right over Kim's head, a rising line drive to center field. Finley races back and does his best Spider-Man, scaling the wall to try for the catch, but everybody knows Peter Parker is a New Yorker and this ball is gone. The game is tied.

Did I mention it was Halloween?

I get three quick groundouts in the tenth.

In the bottom of the inning, Brosius skies one to right for the first out. Sori takes several good hacks before flying out to left. Next up is Derek, who has one hit in the four games and is batting .067 for the Series.

The moon is full and the clock strikes midnight. The Stadium scoreboard flashes, "Welcome to November." With the whole season pushed back a week after September 11, this is the first time baseball has ever been played in November in the big leagues.

Derek goes down 0–2 but works the count and fouls off one ball, then another, then another, clearly trying to knock a ball to right with his trademark inside-out swing.

With the count full, Kim delivers and Derek inside-outs it again, driving the ball down the first base line, a ball that keeps going and going until it just clears the fence in right field. Jeter gives his right-angle fist pump—another trademark—and the Stadium is quaking as we pour out of the dugout for the party at home plate.

It's November 1 and the World Series is tied. I drive home to sleep in my own bed. It's hard to beat this.

Mussina gets a second shot at Arizona in Game 5, and he strikes out six and allows just one hit through four innings. But we haven't been able to get to Miguel Batista, Arizona's starter, either. Then in the fifth, Finley leads off by driving a 1–2 pitch over the wall for the game's first run, and three batters later, catcher Rod Barajas does the same thing.

Batista seems to be getting stronger as the game goes on. I head to the bullpen in the bottom of the sixth.

We sure like to do things the hard way in this World Series, I think.

Mussina stays aggressive, and when Matt Williams pops up with two on and two out in the eighth, a splendid night's work is done. We put two on in the bottom of the frame but don't score, and Ramiro takes over for the ninth. As I warm up in the bullpen, I hear the fans in the bleachers and right-field seats chanting:

Paul O'Neill!
Paul O'Neill!

They have been cheering him all night, knowing that if we don't pull this out, this might be their final chance to let Paulie know how much they have appreciated his play. Paulie has been battling injuries all year. This season could be his last. The chant engulfs us in the pen. The entire Stadium is now chanting his name. I get goose bumps listening to it. Paulie pretends nothing is going on but when Ramiro sets down the Diamondbacks to end the inning, Paulie tips his cap as he leaves the field and the crowd roars in response.

So now we are exactly where we were a night earlier: down two, with Byung-Hyun Kim on the mound. Jorge leads off with a double down the line, but Spencer grounds out and Knoblauch strikes out. It's up to Scott Brosius. He looks at ball one. Kim delivers the 1–0 pitch and Brosius swings. Off goes the ball, deep into the left-field seats. Now Scott Brosius's right fist punches the air.

You can't make this stuff up.

For the second straight night, we are down

by two, down to our last at-bat, and we hit a game-tying two-run homer. As Brosius rounds the bases, Kim is crouched on the mound, like a turtle retreating into its shell. In the TV close-up, he looks as if he might cry. Bob Brenly, the Diamondbacks manager, takes him out in favor of Mike Morgan.

I cruise through an easy tenth, but Morgan cruises, too, retiring seven straight. In the eleventh, I give up two singles, and after a sacrifice, we walk Finley to load the bases. With Johnson looming in Game 6, I know exactly how huge this moment is. I come at Reggie Sanders hard, and get him to line out.

Now the hitter is Mark Grace. I go up 0–2, and that makes all the difference. I can make him try to hit my pitch, and I do, getting him to bounce to third for an inning-ending force.

Twelfth inning: Sterling Hitchcock (traded back to the Yankees from the Padres midseason) relieves me and pitches a scoreless frame. Now Albie Lopez takes the mound for Arizona. Knoblauch singles up the middle;

Brosius bunts him to second. Soriano serves a ball into right for a single, and here comes Knoblauch crossing the plate with the winning run. We win our third straight one-run game. All we need is one more, and a fourth straight world championship is ours.

The Trophy

We are back in the desert for Game 6, and the night turns out to be as pleasant as sitting on a cactus. Going back to 1996, Andy has proven himself as reliable a big-game pitcher as there is, but he doesn't have it tonight, and neither do we. The Diamondbacks score one in the first, three in the second, eight in the third, and three in the fourth. Randy Johnson is on the mound. Another ninth-inning home run is not going to be enough tonight.

The final score is 15–2. The Diamond-backs have twenty-two hits, two more than we had in the first four games of the Series. Ten of the hits come against our long reliever, Jay Witasick, in one and a third innings. I feel for Jay. It's his only appearance in the Series, and his job is to take a beating, to save the other arms in the bullpen in case there's a miraculous comeback. The whole night is about as ugly as it can be, but it's just one loss, so here's how I look at it:

Now it's a best-of-one World Series.

The matchup for Game 7 is right out of a movie script: Two jumbo right-handers, Curt Schilling and Roger Clemens, with a combined record for the year of 42–9.

I don't think this will be a blowout.

Mr. T has already told us how proud he was of us, so he asks Geno Monahan, our trainer, to give the pregame pep talk.

Geno laughs at Mr. T's request, because he doesn't think he's serious.

But it's another inspired idea by Mr. T. Geno is so much more to us than a trainer—somebody who helps our bodies heal and nurtures us through the physical grind of the season. He is as kind and generous a man as you will ever meet. He has been with the Yankees for forty years. The spotlight is never, ever what he wants. But he has it now.

"No matter what happens tonight, guys, you have had some year," Geno says. "From day one of spring training, through 9/11, through two tough series, you've played with such heart. You've played with class and you've been winners—you've been true Yankees. And I've never been prouder to be part of a club, because of what you guys bring every day. Whatever happens out there tonight, you guys are going to walk into this clubhouse and you are going to be the same champions you've been all year. Nothing will change that."

The room is completely silent after Geno finishes, except for the sound of bench coach Don Zimmer crying. A lot of us feel like crying.

Now I want to say a few things.

"This is our game to win," I say. "We just need to trust. Trust in our heart, trust in each other. We are blessed to be here again, to be with each other."

Roger and Schilling both come out in top form. Roger strikes out eight guys in the first four innings, and Schilling matches him, allowing one hit and striking out eight through six.

Finley leads off the bottom of the sixth for the D-Backs with a looping single, then Danny Bautista smokes a fastball to the wall. Finley scores but a brilliant relay throw from Derek nails Bautista as he tries to stretch a hard-hit single into a triple. (Remember the famous baseball advice, kids: Never make the first or last out at third.)

Roger gets out of the inning with just the one run scored and we go to the seventh. Derek singles to lead off. Paulie follows with a single, and then with one out, Tino drives a hard single to right to score Derek and tie the game. Shane almost gets us two more runs, but Finley runs down his line drive and Schilling gets out of the inning without further damage.

The game moves into the eighth. Sori leads off and falls behind, 0–2. He fouls off two pitches and then Schilling delivers a low splitter and Sori golfs it over the left-center-field fence. It's the first time we have the lead in Bank One Ballpark since the first inning of the first game. Moments after Sori's ball lands, the bullpen phone rings.

"Mo, you got the eighth," bullpen coach Rich Monteleone says.

Miguel Batista and then Randy Johnson (Hey, he can sleep for the rest of the week, right?) get the final two outs in relief of Schilling, and I come on for the bottom of the eighth. I go to the back of the mound with the ball in my right hand, close my eyes and say my prayer.

I strike out the side.

Johnson says, "I can do that, too," and sets down Bernie, Tino, and Jorge in order. We have a 2–1 lead. There are three outs left in the season. Three outs separating us from another championship, not just a fourth World Series in a row, but a championship for the people of the city of New York.

Three quick outs and let's get out of here.

I have a powerful sense that we are going to win this game. This is my fifty-second postseason appearance. I have converted twenty-three straight save opportunities and have the lowest ERA of any pitcher in World Series history. I am not overconfident. I just believe that as a team we will finish the job, because we do that as well as any club I've ever seen.

All I think about is throwing the best pitch I can.

The first hitter, Mark Grace, hits a broken-bat looper into center for a single. David

Dellucci pinch-runs for him, extra speed that is important because the next hitter, catcher Damian Miller, is surely bunting. Miller squares and taps his bunt almost straight back to me, an easy force at second. I pounce on it and fire to Derek, but my throw sails into right center field.

It is the second error of my Yankee career.

It is an easy play. I just blow it.

I get back on the rubber. Bank One Ballpark, as quiet as a funeral parlor a minute earlier, now throbs with sound. Mr. T comes out of the dugout. The infielders converge on the mound.

"Let's just get an out—make sure we get one," he says. I hear him, but my mind is elsewhere.

I've just made a terrible play on a bunt and now I am going to make amends.

A pinch hitter, Jay Bell, steps into the box. Bell has the reputation of being a very good bunter, but if I have anything to do with it, these runners will not be advancing.

Bell squares and bunts the first pitch, too hard, to the third-base side. It's not a good bunt, and I am on it, catching it and firing to Scott at third for the force. Scott comes off the bag and holds the ball. Bell may not even be halfway down the first-base line. I am waiting for Scott to throw it across to Tino at first. It is a guaranteed double play, leaving us with two out and a man at second.

But he never throws the ball. Scott is an aggressive, heads-up ballplayer, an excellent third baseman, and a total gamer. Does he have Joe's words—"Make sure we get one"—in mind when he holds the ball? I don't know. I can't worry about it now. The inning is not going the way I expect it to. I can't worry about that, either. I can't start letting negative thoughts seep in. I never deliver a pitch thinking that something bad is going to happen.

There are runners at first and second, with one out. There is a batter to get out. That's all that I am focused on—Tony Womack, the Diamondbacks slap-hitting shortstop. Womack settles into the batter's box. If I throw my best cutter, I know I can saw him off, get either a strikeout or a broken bat. I throw a cutter up for a ball, and then another, to fall behind, 2–0. My command is not there. I am not hitting my spots. I battle back to 2–2 and fire another cutter at Womack, but it's not inside enough, and he doubles to right field, tying the game with runners still on at second and third.

The crowd is in full frenzy now, tasting victory, sweeter that it's coming against the mighty Yankees and their supposedly invincible closer.

I am not giving up.

Ever.

The next hitter is Craig Counsell. On an 0–1 pitch, my cutter bores in on him. He starts to swing but stops. The ball hits him on the right hand.

The bases are loaded.

I take a deep breath.

Luis Gonzalez is up again, the Diamondbacks' best hitter. In two previous at-bats in the Series I have struck him out and got him to hit a weak grounder. He has a wide-open stance. Mr. T has ordered the infield in to get the run at the plate, not wanting to risk a weak grounder that could end the World Series. Gonzalez hasn't made good contact off of me, so he chokes up on the bat. Later I find out it is the first time he has choked up all year.

Make a good pitch, get an out—these are my thoughts. I am calm. Focused. I am going to get him.

Gonzalez fouls off my first cutter, and then I fire another one, a good one, a pitch that veers hard into his hands. Gonzalez swings. He breaks his bat. The ball pops into the air, toward shortstop. I see its trajectory and know it is heading for the edge of the grass behind Derek.

I know it is trouble.

In his normal position, Derek backpedals a few steps and makes the play. But he is not in his normal position.

The ball plops a foot or two beyond the infield dirt. Jay Bell races home.

There are no more pitches to make.

The Arizona Diamondbacks are world champions.

I walk off the field as the Diamondbacks are pouring onto it. I am in something close to shock. Never could I have envisioned this ending.

I walk into the dugout, down the steps, up into the clubhouse. Jorge comes by and pats my back. I get a lot of pats on the back. I don't remember if anybody says anything to me.

I sit at my locker for a long time afterward. "I don't know what happened," I tell Mr. T. "I knew we were winning that game. I don't understand it. I lost the game. But look at how it happened. Look at all the things that occurred that were so bizarre."

I talk to the press, answer all the questions, take the blame. Yes, I threw the pitches I wanted. No, I don't remember the last time I threw away a bunt like that. Yes, I got

Gonzalez to hit my pitch, but he fought it off and was able to make contact. I speak softly. I do not throw anything or kick anything. But I am hurting. I have done my best, sure. But my best is not good enough. I have let down the team. That is what hurts most. My teammates are counting on me and I do not come through.

After I shower and change, I find Clara outside the clubhouse. She rubs my back tenderly. It is more comforting to me than any words can be. I take her hand and we walk to the bus. I have tears in my eyes. The guys on the team are there for me, I know that, but they are giving me space. We get to the airport. The tears do not stop. They don't stop for the whole trip across the country.

Clara is right next to me, as she has been since I was a boy. Even in my sorrow, I am so thankful for my wife and the love the Lord has surrounded me with. We land in New York and we drive home. It is five o'clock in the morning. The sun is not yet up.

Outside the door to our bedroom, I see something on the floor. I bend to pick it up. It is a small trophy, probably eight inches high, with a wooden base and the golden likeness of a ball-player above it. It is a Little League trophy. It belongs to our oldest son, Mariano Jr., who has just turned eight.

I hold it close, not smiling but feeling something much deeper.

The Curse of the Bambino

It is a raw Saturday in April, the first week of the 2002 season. We are playing the Tampa Bay Devil Rays (that was still their name then) in the Bronx. I have had to make peace with the way the 2001 World Series ended, but it has been hard. The only way is to recommit myself to living in the present.

I am at my locker in the clubhouse, starting

to get dressed, thinking about the new season, a new beginning, and how lucky I am to wear this uniform, how much I cherish wearing it.

For me, putting on the Yankee uniform every day is a thrill. You hear guys who sign with the Yankees talk about how great it feels to be putting on the pinstripes. I completely understand. It is about the history of the uniform, the dignity and the championships, the way it stands for enduring excellence. Maybe it's because I am from a fishing village that is one stop from the end of the earth that the Yankee uniform means so much. I just know I never take it for granted.

I always take my time getting dressed because I want to savor it. Jorge teases that it takes me so long because I am fanatical about aligning the pinstripes of the pants with the pinstripes of the shirt. I don't really do that, but he's only exaggerating a little.

The uniform may be timeless, but there is more change around the Yankees this season than any year since I arrived. Paul O'Neill retires, and so does Scott Brosius. Tino Martinez is now a Cardinal, and Chuck Knoblauch is a Royal and retires himself after 2002, his throwing problem ending his career prematurely. Jason Giambi, our big free-agent signing, is now our first baseman. David Wells is back and we've also added Robin Ventura, Steve Karsay, and Rondell White. It is another stellar season, with 103 victories, but it's also the most frustrating season of my career. I make three trips to the disabled list and pitch in the fewest games (forty-five) of any year since 1995, when I was up and down from Columbus. Not playing is not easy for me. I can't shag batting practice fly balls. I can't pitch. I take pride in being someone my teammates can count on. I rest and get treatment, but I am not a good patient. I am not very good at *being* patient, either.

Just ask Clara.

I'm doing more watching and waiting this season than I want, but another first-place finish in the American League East earns us a best-of-five division series against the Angels. They are the best-hitting team in baseball, a young club that won ninety-nine games one year after winning just seventy-five. We have been crushing home runs all year, and in Game 1, at Yankee Stadium, Derek, Giambi, Rondell White, and Bernie all hit balls out of the park. Roger and Ramiro get slapped around a bit, but I get the save in an 8–5 victory.

We rally from an early 4–0 deficit in Game 2 to go up, 5–4, but then the Angels homer late to win, 8–6.

The series shifts to Anaheim, and we jump out to a 6–1 lead after two and a half innings, but here come the Angels again, getting three more hits, including a homer from Adam Kennedy and a homer and four RBIs from Tim Salmon. They roll to a 9–6 victory.

We are one game away from getting bounced

out of the playoffs earlier than we have in our entire championship era.

By the time the Angels put on a parade worthy of Disneyland in a seven-hit, eight-run fifth inning against David Wells in Game 4, we are basically done. The final score is 9–5. The Angels hit .376 for the series and come from behind in all three victories. They are relentless, and their bullpen dominates ours. Their grittiness reminds me of the way we played when we were winning championships. You can win all the games you want in the regular season, but when your postseason ends in four games it is impossible to feel good about the year.

Our third son is named Jaziel, which means "strength of God." He is born seven weeks after our season ends, a healthy nine-pound boy. All goes fine for him but Clara has complications that require immediate surgery. I

am in the delivery room when her doctor real-
izes this and it scares me. It is terrifying to see
my strong wife suddenly so vulnerable.

I told you I don't often pray for results, but
I was praying for them then.

Mercifully, Clara recovers.

Our first off-season as a family of five passes
in a snap, and it is time to go to spring training for the 2003 season, where all kinds of
unforeseen things will happen. On opening
day, Derek slams into the shin guards of the
Toronto Blue Jays' catcher; he's out for six
weeks. I miss the first twenty-five games of
the season when a groin problem resurfaces
during one of my last spring training games.
We start by going 23–6, but then go 11–17
in May. We finish tied with the Braves for
the best record in baseball (101–61), and yet
we lose eleven out of twelve in our own ballpark at one point, and somehow get no-hit by

six Houston Astros pitchers—the first time a Yankees team has been no-hit since 1958.

Who ever heard of getting no-hit by six pitchers?

But by the time October arrives, I have a much better feeling about things. We take out the Twins in four games in the division series, and I retire all twelve batters I face. Now it is time for the Yankees and the Red Sox, best of seven for the American League pennant.

The Red Sox, who have played us tough all year, are convinced this is their year, and they take Game 1 behind the knuckleballer Tim Wakefield and home runs from David Ortiz, Manny Ramírez, and Todd Walker. Andy gets us even in Game 2, pitching into the seventh, before giving way to José Contreras and me in a 6–2 triumph, sending us up to Fenway for a Game 3 matchup between Roger Clemens and Pedro Martínez. It's supposed to be Roger's last game in Fenway, and even as he warms up, the atmosphere feels electric.

Manny Ramírez hits a two-run single to

give Pedro a lead in the bottom of the first, but in the third, Derek drives a hanging curveball onto Lansdowne Street, clear over the huge left-field wall, known to Sox fans as "The Green Monster." We rally again in the fourth when Hideki Matsui, playing in his first Yankee–Red Sox postseason series, rifles a double to right.

Karim García, our right fielder, steps in. He already has an RBI single off Pedro. Pedro's first pitch is a fastball behind García's head, hitting him in the upper back. García is furious; he glares at Pedro and curses him out. Pedro curses right back. Our bench is up. The Red Sox bench is up. One play later, on a 6-4-3 double-play ball, García overruns second and takes out Walker, the Sox second baseman. It's a dirty play, and Walker is rightfully steamed. Now García has words with Pedro as he heads off, both benches are on the steps, and nobody is giving Pedro more of an earful than Jorge.

They don't like each other, and in the

playoffs, fuses are shorter. Pedro stares and points at Jorge, and then points to his head, twice. I am watching on the clubhouse TV and am disturbed by Pedro's antics. He's too good a pitcher to act like this. First he head-hunts García, and now he inflames things even more by suggesting he's going to drill Jorge in the head.

If somebody rubs two sticks together this whole place could explode, I think.

Sure enough, just a few minutes later, in the bottom of the fourth, Roger throws a high fastball, slightly inside, to Manny Ramírez. The pitch isn't close to hitting him, but Manny brandishes his bat and starts holler-ing and walking toward Roger, and now the benches empty. While everybody else heads for the mound, Don Zimmer, our rotund, seventy-two-year-old bench coach, takes off for the Sox dugout—Pedro Martínez is stand-ing in front of it. Pedro sees Zimmer coming at him like a round little bull. Zimmer raises his left arm and Pedro steps back as if he were a matador, shoving Zimmer to the ground. Zim's hat falls off and he suffers a little cut, and everybody is gathering around him to make sure he's okay.

How much lower can Pedro go? I wonder.

Zim is totally wrong to bull-rush Pedro, but you can't throw an old man on the ground. You just cannot.

I don't let this mayhem get into my head. I stay calm, even though I haven't done well against the Red Sox this year; I've blown two saves and they have sixteen hits against me in ten innings. As much as I appreciate Fenway's charms, the mound is one of my least favorite in the league. The clay is on the soft side, so by the time I get out there, often after two hundred or so pitches have been thrown, it's pretty roughed up and doesn't have the hard landing spots I prefer. But none of that matters. You compete where you have to compete. The mound is soft?

Deal with it, Mo.

I run in from the pen and warm up with

Jorge. We have been together for nine years now, and he isn't just a close friend, he's a soul mate, a guy I am in total sync with. He knows what I like, how I think, that I want to keep things simple. He knows I will never shake my head if I want to change a pitch or a location. All I will do is keep looking in. If I keep looking in, then he knows I want to throw something else.

But who is kidding whom? I throw the cutter 90 percent of the time. For most pitchers, a catcher puts down one finger for a fastball, two for a curve, three for a slider, and so on. With me, one is a cutter, and two is a two-seam fastball. If there is a runner on second, four is a cutter and two is a two-seamer. If Jorge waggles his fingers as he puts them down, he wants the pitch up.

That's the sum total of our signs.

Jorge puts down one finger almost exclusively at the end of Game 3. I face six Red Sox hitters and retire them on nineteen pitches. We win, 4–3, and take a 2–1 lead in the series, but this is Red Sox–Yankees. I have a feeling this is going the distance, and that is exactly what happens. We win Games 2, 3, and 5. The Red Sox win Games 1, 4, and 6.

Game 7 is at the Stadium, Pedro vs. Roger, Part II.

Pedro is much sharper than he was in Game 3, and Roger gets knocked around: three runs in the third; a leadoff homer to Kevin Millar in the fourth. A walk and a single follow, and Mr. T has seen enough, calling for Mussina, who has never thrown a pitch of relief in his career. He strikes out Jason Varitek on three pitches, and then gets Johnny Damon to hit into a double play. Mussina has already lost two games in the series and given up five home runs; these are the most important outs he's gotten as a Yankee, and he doesn't stop there. He strikes out David Ortiz with two men on an inning later.

He's getting every single out he has to have,
I think.

In all, Mussina throws three scoreless
innings, giving our bats time to wake up.
Giambi belts Pedro's first pitch of the fifth
inning, a changeup away, over the center-field
fence, making it 4–1. It is only our third hit of
the night.

Next time up Giambi gets a fastball away,
which he deposits over the wall in straightaway center. Now it's 4–2, and when Enrique
Wilson legs out an infield single and García
ropes a single to right, there's more positive
energy in the Stadium than there has been all
night.

Then Pedro strikes out Sori for the fourth
time, and the energy drains right back out.
Pedro points his finger to the sky, his trademark sign-off, and gets a hug from Nomar
Garciaparra in the dugout. We all figure he's
done. Pedro assumes he's done, but his manager, Grady Little, asks: "Can you give me
one more inning?" Pedro says okay, even

though he clearly thought his night was over. Ortiz homers off of Wells, another emergency reliever, to make it 5–2, and we have six outs left.

Pedro comes back out for the eighth. With one out, Derek hits an 0–2 pitch to right that Trot Nixon misplays, the ball bouncing just over his glove for a double. Bernie drives a single to center to score Derek, and then Matsui drills a ground-rule double to right. Still, Little leaves Pedro in. Jorge hits a flare to center, and it falls in. The game is tied. The Stadium erupts. Pedro exits. The frenzy and noise are overwhelming, and so are my emotions.

I put down my glove, leave the bullpen, and run up a small flight of stairs, where there is a bench and a bathroom. I go into the bathroom, close the door, and cry.

The moment is just too much for me.

We are down by three to Pedro Martínez with five outs to go and now the game is tied. I say a prayer because that is what I do in moments like this. It calms me.

I let the tears come for a minute or two, wipe them away, and finish my warm-up.

The Sox bullpen does the job and I come in for a fairly routine top of the ninth, ending it by getting Todd Walker to hit a little looper to second with one man on. When it leaves his bat, I crouch to watch it, worried it might be another soft hit with terrible consequences. But Sori jumps to make the catch, and I jump on the mound when he does.

Mike Timlin sets us down in order in the ninth, and with two outs in the tenth, Ortiz takes me the other way with a double off the wall, but I escape by popping up Kevin Millar.

After Tim Wakefield and his knuckleball put us away in order in the bottom of the tenth, I have my own 1-2-3 inning, with two strikeouts. It's my first three-inning outing in seven years. When I get to the dugout, Mel comes up to me.

"Great job, Mo," he says.

"I can give you another," I say.

Mel doesn't want me going out there again, I'm sure. But there is no way I am coming out of the game. If I need to pitch a fourth inning, I am going to do it. A fifth inning? I will throw that, too. The season is just about over. I have a long time to rest. I don't want to stay in the game. I have to. It is my duty. I am not going to let Mr. T give the ball to anybody else.

Aaron Boone leads off the bottom of the eleventh. He is hitting .125 for the series. Wakefield's first pitch is a knuckler that comes in about waist-high, on the inner half. Boone turns on it, and the minute he does, we know. Everybody in the Stadium knows—you can tell by the roar. The ball lands a dozen or more rows deep.

We are going back to the World Series.

The whole team pours out of the dugout to greet Aaron at home, but I have a different destination.

I am running to the pitcher's mound. I need to be on the pitcher's mound. I get there just as Aaron rounds second and heads to third. I am on my hands and knees, saying a prayer of gratitude, crying in the dirt.

Lee Mazzilli, our first-base coach, follows me to the mound and puts his arms around me as I weep. All around me guys are hugging. I am weeping. I am not sure where these deep emotions are coming from. Is it because I felt like I had failed my team in our last Game 7, two years before?

I don't know. It doesn't matter.

When I get to my feet, I share a hug with Aaron and then a long embrace with Mr. T.

I am named MVP of the American League Championship Series, but the trophy should be divided twenty-five ways. That is not a throwaway line. It's the truth.

We are a band of brothers. We never stop battling.

NOTES FROM MO

The Steal of the Century

Baseball is full of stories about bad trades, including the deal between the Mets and the Cleveland Indians in which the Mets agreed to take third baseman Harry Chiti for a "player to be named later." They watched Chiti play for a while, and then decided the player they'd send back to the Indians was...Harry Chiti.

But most people agree the deal that sent Babe Ruth from Boston to New York was one of the worst—and most fateful—trades in baseball history.

The Babe joined the Boston Red Sox in 1914, and won sixty-five games as a pitcher in his first three years, before his transformation into an outfielder—and one of the most feared hitters of all time. His towering home runs made him a national sensation.

During his five seasons with the Sox (1914–1919), the team won three World Series titles.

Then, in 1920, Sox owner Harry Frazee sold Ruth's contract to the Yankees for $100,000 and a $300,000 loan, because he needed cash to invest in another business interest: Broadway musicals.

Sportswriters called it "the steal of the century." Before Ruth's arrival, the Yankees had never won a World Series. After he put on the pinstripes, the Yankees won a staggering twenty-six titles, including four when Babe was with the team.

The Red Sox's fortunes headed the other way. After they let Babe go, the Red Sox didn't win another World Series for *eighty-six years*, a near century of bad luck chalked up to the "Curse of the Bambino," cosmic payback for having sold one of the best players in baseball history to an archrival. The idea of a curse was cemented in 1986. The Sox were up by two runs and one out away from finally winning the World Series when the New York Mets' Mookie Wilson hit a ball that squirted through Boston first baseman Bill Buckner's legs, allowing the winning run to score. The Mets went on to win the game, and their second World Series title.

The Red Sox had to keep waiting.

Fish Bait

In the first inning of Game 3 of the World Series against the Florida Marlins, Josh Beckett, a twenty-three-year-old kid with a wicked fastball and a curveball to match, strikes out Derek on three pitches. Derek spends the next three hours and eight innings making sure we win the game. As I watch him do this, I realize it has been ten years since we were teammates in Greensboro, the year he made fifty-six errors and still I knew he was going to be a great ballplayer.

What I saw in Greensboro is the same thing I see now: a man with an insatiable desire to win. Derek's résumé of big moments is staggering. The double that started the rally against Pedro in Game 3. The flip play. The home run in the tenth inning of Game 4 to beat the Diamondbacks in 2001. The leadoff homer in Game 4 against the Mets in 2000. The hit that started the big rally in Game 4 against the Braves, the one that culminated with Jim Leyritz's home run.

Now he is putting on a show in Game 3 against Beckett and the Fish, an expansion team that formed in 1993 and has already, improbably, won a World Series, beating Cleveland in 1997. The sportswriters are predicting this will be a lopsided win for us—a mismatch in star power, payroll, and tradition. We split the first two games in New York and know beating Beckett tonight can alter the course of the whole Series. So after that initial strikeout, here is what happens:

Derek doubles to left and scores in the

fourth. He singles to center to lead off the sixth. He doubles to right and scores the go-ahead run in the eighth.

Beckett pitches into the seventh and strikes out ten, giving up just three hits and two runs, all to Derek.

I am warming up, getting ready to come on for Mussina, who is superb all night. Minutes after Derek's third hit and second run knocks Beckett out of the game, I am on the mound, throwing six pitches to retire Pudge Rodríguez, Miguel Cabrera, and Derrek Lee. We explode for four more runs on homers from Aaron Boone and Bernie, then shut down the Marlins to seal the win.

We've beaten the Marlins' best pitcher and have Roger Clemens going in Game 4, and David Wells in Game 5. Nobody is taking anything for granted, but I like our chances. When Rubén Sierra laces a two-out, two-run triple down the right-field line in the ninth inning to tie Game 4 at 3–3, it seems familiar, just another Yankee workday in October.

It's a hit straight out of 1996 or 1998 or 2000, I think.

But from that point on, very little goes right for the Yankees in the 2003 World Series. As much as it stings to think about, the truth is undeniable: We are not the same team we used to be. Not even close. The Marlins are fast and aggressive and play with spunk, but those Yankee teams that won four World Series in five years would've hammered them, because those were guys who cared more about winning than anything else. It's just not like that anymore.

We leave the bases loaded in the top of the eleventh, and then watch as Alex Gonzalez, the Marlins shortstop, hits a walk-off home run in the bottom of the twelfth. It's a highlight right out of the Aaron Boone playbook, only now we are on the receiving end.

So the Series is tied at two games apiece. Game 5 unspools faster than a runaway fishing line. We get one hit in eight at-bats with runners in scoring position. It adds up to a 6–4 defeat. We go back to Yankee Stadium, where Andy pitches really well, but Josh Beckett pitches even better, spinning a five-hit shutout and striking out nine, on three days' rest. We whimper off to clear out our lockers, to another off-season that doesn't include a parade.

Anything short of a championship tends to result in big changes for George Steinbrenner's Yankees, and 2004 brings about the biggest change you can have: the acquisition of Alex Rodriguez, the American League MVP, a man widely considered the best player in baseball. Alfonso Soriano goes to the Texas Rangers in the deal, and Alex, deferring to Derek, goes to third base from his natural position of shortstop. It's Alex's third team in four seasons, and I'm thrilled we have him, but as I look ahead to my own 2004 season, the final year of my contract with the Yankees, I have an overwhelming desire to not chase the biggest contract I can. I do not want to wear another uniform. I have no interest in playing the free-agent game, posturing about how I might be on my way someplace else.

Maybe it costs me money. A few years later, the Phillies offer me a contract for much more money than what the Yankees offer. Do you know how long I consider that? For about half the time it takes you to read this page. The reason is very simple:

I have never played the game for money. I am fortunate to be able to provide well for my family, but it has never been my motivation for playing. I always felt that if I worked hard and tried to be a good teammate, the money aspect would take care of itself, and that is exactly what has happened. There hasn't been one time in my career when I looked at what somebody else was earning and felt shortchanged. It would make me unhappy, tying my contentment to the size of my bank account. I don't need anything but the love of the people who matter to me.

Curse Reversed

It's opening day in Boston, April 11, 2005, and I am more popular than Paul Revere. The Boston Red Sox—the *world champion* Boston Red Sox—are getting their 2004 World Series rings and hoisting their championship flag, and, what a coincidence, the New York Yankees are in town for the occasion. One by one, we are introduced. Everybody gets booed, some more than others, Alex Rodriguez most of all. After Randy

Johnson, No. 41, gets his booing, it is my turn.

The public address announcer says:

Number 42, Mariano Rivera...

The Fenway Park crowd goes nuts, people standing and cheering as I run onto the field, taking my spot next to Chien-Ming Wang and Randy. I remove my cap and bow. I laugh, and laugh some more, and the cheer keeps going, as if I were one of their own. Of course, I know I don't rank with Ortiz or Damon in their hearts. I am being saluted for my contributions to the Red Sox's first world championship title in eighty-six years.

Curse reversed.

We won our division in 2004, but the Red Sox were right on our heels, taking second place and the wild-card spot. We had little trouble with the Twins in the division series but the Sox had even less with Anaheim, sweeping their series 3–0.

Still, we have things in hand in the ALCS, taking the first two games at home. Off we go to Boston, but Red Sox hopes that the sight of the Green Monster will change their fortunes get buried beneath an avalanche of Yankee home runs. Matsui hits two of them and goes five for six with five RBIs. Alex Rodriguez has another, drives in three, and scores five. Gary Sheffield homers and has four hits, and Bernie has four hits, too. It's a nightlong batting practice session and a 19–8 triumph for us. With El Duque matched against Derek Lowe in Game 4, it doesn't even look as if it will be a fair fight.

We hold to a 4–3 lead through seven innings of Game 4. The bullpen phone rings.

"Mo, you got the eighth," Rich Monteleone says.

Manny Ramirez singles, but I strike out Ortiz and get through the heart of the Sox order with no drama.

In the ninth, the leadoff batter is Millar. He has had success against me, so I am extra careful. My 3–1 pitch is high and Millar walks, and is immediately replaced by Dave Roberts, who is in the game to steal a base. I know it. Jorge knows it. The whole park knows it. Roberts stole thirty-eight bases in forty-one tries this season. I throw to first several times to keep him close. On my first pitch to the next hitter, Bill Mueller, Roberts is off. Jorge makes a strong throw to Derek, who slaps on the tag an instant late. Roberts is in scoring position with nobody out.

I throw a cutter to Mueller, not where I want it, and he spanks it up the middle. I try to spear it like a hockey goalie, but the ball goes into center and Dave Roberts goes home.

Save blown. Game tied.

The fans in Fenway love it. I get out of the inning, but the damage is done. In the bottom of the twelfth, Ortiz, also known as Big Papi, also known as the hottest hitter on earth through these playoffs, blasts a two-run homer.

The game lasts five hours and two minutes, and it not only gives the Red Sox a win, it gives them hope. In Game 5, we're up, 4–2, in the eighth and lose in fourteen innings. We come back to the Bronx in Game 6, Schilling out-pitches Lieber, and we lose, 4–2. With each passing inning, we look tighter than spandex on the Pillsbury Doughboy.

The Red Sox complete the greatest come-back in postseason baseball history with a 10–3 drubbing in Game 7. Nobody feels worse about it than I do. I am the one who left the door ajar, blowing the save in Game 4.

The Sox go on to sweep the St. Louis Car-dinals in the World Series, ending an eighty-six-year drought. So on the day the team gets their rings, their fans are beyond happy, and I am willing to play along. It is the greatest cele-bration Boston has had in a long time, and it's doubly sweet that their victory included mak-ing a historic comeback against their fiercest rivals—us.

Let them rejoice. I will be doing all I can to get them out the next time, and perhaps make myself a bit less popular around town.

I have bigger matters to be concerned about than ovations in enemy ballparks as the 2005 season begins. The main one is getting booed in my own ballpark. I blow back-to-back saves against, yes, the Red Sox, during our opening home stand, and in the second one, I am so ineffective (three walks, three singles, five runs) that Mr. T comes to get me, earning me a resounding Bronx cheer on my trip to the dugout. Some of my teammates are appalled that I get booed, but I don't expect a lifetime pass because I've had a lot of saves.

I turn my attention to improving the performance that triggers the booing. My issue is not having my usual command—a result, I'm sure, of the elbow tenderness that cost me time during the spring. I count on hitting spots, especially against the Red Sox, a patient team that sees me so much that it's hard to surprise them with anything. In the outing that gets me booed, I throw thirty-eight pitches and only eighteen are strikes. If that's not the worst ball–strike ratio of my career, I'd be surprised. I know it's a question of fine-tuning things. If I throw more, and tighten up my delivery, the results will be there.

I convert my next thirty-one save opportunities—a stretch of more than four months. One of the appearances comes in Detroit in early July, in a game that does my heart good. Bernie Williams, now thirty-six, is being phased out as the regular center fielder. In a recent series against the Mets, we lose two of three at Yankee Stadium. Bernie drops a fly ball in one game, lets a runner advance in another, and gets run on, repeatedly. Mr. T says he wants to give Bernie a couple of days off to clear his head. Bernie doesn't want time off but gets it anyway.

You can't call Bernie an unsung hero, not when he set the record (eighty) for postseason RBIs. He has won a batting title and driven in more than a hundred runs in a season five times.

Not that you will hear Bernie touting these numbers. He is a gentle soul, a sensitive guy whose disposition is more like an artist's than a star athlete's. Ten minutes before first pitch, you would always find him in the clubhouse, strumming chords on his guitar, as if that were going to be his main activity for the night.

But this season has not been easy for Bernie. The Yankees are about to bring up Melky Cabrera to play center field, and more and more, Bernie is either a DH or nothing. Every athlete gets older, but that doesn't make it any easier to watch when a player has been such a champion.

We're only a .500 team (39–39) when we head into Comerica Park that afternoon, Mussina going against Sean Douglass, a six-foot-six right-hander.

Bernie singles in the fourth, the 2,154th hit of his career, moving him past Don Mattingly on the Yankee hits list, behind only the Big Four: Lou Gehrig, Babe Ruth, Mickey Mantle, and Joe DiMaggio. Then he belts a line-drive single to bring home two runs in the sixth. He hits another single in the eighth, and in the ninth, breaks open a one-run game with a three-run home run.

Bernie is undeniably the star of the game. And when the press comes to the clubhouse to talk to him, he is already gone. He has been a special teammate and a big-time player for the Yankees for a long time. I am happy to see him have such a huge day.

With the way the season started, getting hailed as a hero in Boston and botching those first two save chances against the Sox, I can't imagine a better way to finish it off than being back in Fenway Park to clinch another AL East title. I decide it's time for another dugout appearance. "Let's finish the job right now," I say. "This is our division. Let's leave it all out there today."

The guys always seem amused when I go into cheerleader mode. I have no problem amusing them if it produces the desired result. Alex, Gary Sheffield, and Matsui all launch homers, and Randy Johnson pitches into the eighth. For Alex, it's home run No. 48 in an MVP season. When Johnny Damon swings and hits a ball back to me with two out in the ninth, we are AL East champions for the ninth straight season. The Red Sox finish with the same 95–67 record as we do, but we win the division because we won the season series against them.

We draw the Angels in the division series and fly to Anaheim for the first two games. We take the first, knocking Bartolo Colón around early, thanks to a first-inning, three-run double by our rookie second baseman, Robinson Canó. We kick away a prime chance to take a two-game lead by making three errors in Game 2. Still, we're even as we head back to New York, and we have Randy Johnson, future Hall of Famer, matched up against Paul Byrd.

Byrd doesn't have it, but Randy is worse. He gives up nine hits and five runs in three innings. Still, we climb out of a five-run hole to take a 6–5 lead, which the bullpen can't hold. We lose, 11–7.

Now we're down, two games to one.

We fight back to win Game 4. I get the final six outs, but the best part is the outpouring of love for Bernie, who gets four standing ovations and has his name chanted over and over again, the same way Paul O'Neill's was four years earlier. It's not at all certain Bernie will be back next year. Yankee fans make sure he gets a proper goodbye.

We fall behind in Game 5 but Derek leads off the seventh with a home run to cut their lead to two. We still have nine outs to go. We've come back when things have looked bleak before. Think about Game 7 against Pedro, just two years ago, down three in the eighth. We can do it again.

Alex grounds out, Sheffield flies out, and Matsui pops out.

We don't do anything in the eighth, either.

In the ninth, Derek leads off with a single, but Alex hits into a double play. Giambi and Sheffield single, and then Matsui hits a shot wide of first that Darin Erstad makes a great play on, throwing to Francisco Rodríguez for the final out.

It's my least favorite kind of game, the kind where the call to the bullpen to "get Mo up" never comes. It's a helpless, hollow feeling, wanting to compete, and never getting the chance.

21

The Numbers Game

Numbers mean very little to me. Much as I'd like to blame it on Mrs. Tejada, my old math teacher, I can't. I play a sport that is obsessed with statistics, churning out enough numbers to fill a barge. Me? I would be a terrible guy to have as your fantasy advisor. You know when I know about a milestone? When somebody tells me about it.

In June 2006, I have a five-pitch, three-out save in Fenway. (Can you believe it? They didn't cheer!) It's No. 391 of my career, moving me past Dennis Eckersley into fourth place on the all-time saves list.

Six weeks later, I throw two scoreless innings at Yankee Stadium against the White Sox for save No. 400. On September 15, 2008, also against the White Sox, I save a win for Phil Coke. That's save No. 479, moving me past Lee Smith for second on the all-time list.

If reporters didn't keep asking me about it, I wouldn't know where I stood on the all-time saves list. But it's different when I pass Trevor Hoffman's 601 saves, because it's a big topic all over the media.

What these milestones mean to me could not be simpler: I am doing my job—and we are winning ball games.

I hear stories over the years about closers—some big-name closers—who refuse to go into the game if it is not a save situation.

"Sorry, Skip, I can't get loose," they might say. Or: "I don't think I can give you anything today." In other words, "If it's not helping my stats, I'm not taking the ball."

If I were the manager of a pitcher with that attitude, I'd get rid of the guy in a heartbeat. If all that concerns you is your own career, go play tennis or golf.

Early in September 2007, we are in a pennant and wild-card race and we have an eight-run lead against the Mariners, not a save opportunity. Mr. T brings me in to get the final three outs. In the final moments of our collapse and the Game 7 defeat to the Red Sox in the 2004 ALCS, Mr. T asked me to get the third out in a 10–3 loss game that represents one of the sorriest nights in Yankee history.

You know what I am thinking?

My manager wants me to pitch, I pitch.

I can't imagine not taking the ball, ever.

So *my* numbers? Unless you are talking about my *team's* numbers, I am not too interested.

From start to finish in 2006, we put up team numbers that would make a calculator smoke. We score 930 runs for the season, 60 more than the next closest team. We clobber 210 home runs, and with a lineup that includes Rodriguez, Jeter, Sheffield, Posada, Abreu, Canó, Williams, Giambi, Matsui, and ex–Red Sox Johnny Damon, who switched sides when he signed with us in 2006, it's a wonder we don't score ten runs a game.

We finish with ninety-seven victories and end the regular season at home before the usual 50,000 fans and with a new manager, Bernie Williams. Bernie is playing his final regular-season game and with the division title clinched, Mr. T continues his tradition of letting a player manage the final game. This year, it's Bernie's turn.

For a shy musician, Bernie is a brilliant manager. Derek is battling the Twins' Joe Mauer for the batting title. When Derek singles in the first, he is only half a point behind. But Mauer winds up getting two hits, and when it's clear Derek can't catch him, Bernie sends a minor league call-up, Andy Cannizaro, No. 63, out to replace Derek in the ninth. Derek points to his chest, as if to say, *Me?* He leaves to a huge ovation. Later, in the ninth, Bernie pinch-hits himself and doubles to center. The first-base coach, Tony Pena, makes sure to retrieve the ball—it turns out to be Bernie's 2,336th and final hit—and tosses it into the dugout, where Jorge grabs it, looks at Bernie on second, and pretends to heave the ball into the stands.

One sour note is sounded when Bernie brings in Kyle Farnsworth, who unfortunately gives up a two-run homer in the ninth, the difference in a 7–5 loss. In his postgame press conference, conducted in Mr. T's chair, Bernie announces that George Steinbrenner has fired him.

It's all good fun, and we are upbeat going into the division series against the Tigers, who lose 31 of their last 50 games but still find a way to win 95, up from 71 the year before. Pitching has always been the core of our championship teams, so I am not completely sold on the idea that we can just bludgeon teams out of our way with our bats. But plenty of people do think that, including Al Kaline, the Tigers' Hall of Fame outfielder, a man who played against Mickey Mantle and the great Yankee teams of the 1950s and early '60s and says he thinks this Yankee lineup is deeper and better. The big-bat formula works fine to begin the series, as Derek homers while going 5 for 5. Giambi homers, Bobby Abreu has four RBIs, and we bang out fourteen hits. I save an 8–4 decision for Chien-Ming Wang, and when Damon clocks a three-run blast off of Justin Verlander early in Game 2 to give Mussina a 3–1 lead, I think we're in a good place. But the Tigers have the best pitching staff in the majors, and if the old cliché that good pitching stops good hitting seemed like a joke in Game 1, nobody is laughing now. We leave seven men in scoring position, wasting all kinds of great opportunities.

Alex is already upset that he's batting sixth instead of cleanup, and I can't say I understand Mr. T's thinking there. Alex hit 36 homers and drove in 121 runs batting cleanup, and even though that's a down year for him and he has slumped in the postseason the last two years, he was in a great groove going into the playoffs. I don't know whether Mr. T is looking to take the pressure off Alex or using the demotion to motivate him. "Don't worry about it," I tell him. "Just go out and hit the way you can and everything will take care of itself."

Alex is a very proud man, though. Appearances are important to him. Being the cleanup hitter is important to him. He hasn't hit this low in a lineup since his first full year with the Mariners ten years earlier.

We lose Game 2 by a run. Series tied at one game all.

Alex is back in the cleanup spot in Game 3 in Detroit, but it doesn't change the results. Kenny Rogers, a member of our '96 championship team, hasn't beaten a Yankee team in a dozen years, but he gives up only five hits, strikes out eight, and exits in the eighth with a 6–0 lead that holds up.

What is it with these division series? Why do we seem to be in a fight for our playoff lives every year? I haven't pitched since the first game of the series, and that is not part of our game plan. But I am forever optimistic. All we have to do is win a game. That's it. Win Saturday, and then we have a deciding Game 5 at home, with our best starter, Wang, on the hill. We put up one good at-bat, then another. We throw one good pitch, then another. We keep battling. That is the championship recipe. Winning all the little battles allows you to win the greater one.

The Tigers do these things superbly. The Yankees? Not so much. With our season on the line, we can't get anything going. Alex, now hitting in the eight hole, looks lost, and so do plenty of others up and down the lineup. Jeremy Bonderman, the Tigers' hard-throwing starter, pitches a perfect game through five. Our starter, Jaret Wright, gives up two homers to fall behind, 3–0, in the second, then gives up an unearned run in the fourth after Alex makes an error. The lead grows to 8–0, and we only get to 8–3 because Jorge, who hits .500 for the series, hits a two-run homer with two outs in the ninth off of reliever Jamie Walker.

The Yankee highlights are otherwise nonexistent. Alex finishes the series with an average of .071 (1 for 14) and no RBIs. He's not alone. Sheffield hits .083, and, as a team, we get two hits in our last twenty-one at-bats with runners in scoring position. For years we win with top-notch pitching and a lockdown bullpen, and one clutch hit after another. We don't have stars all over the field; we just have guys who grind and pull it out.

Even I can keep track of the numbers in this series. I throw twelve pitches and complete one inning.

Season over.

Spring may bring renewal, but when I report to Tampa in 2007 it also brings sadness. Bernie Williams won't be in camp. He wants to return to a part-time role similar to what he did very well in 2006, for very little money. The Yankees are not interested. They tell Bernie he can come to camp, but only as a minor league invitee, not with a major league deal. For Bernie, a four-time world champion who has been a Yankee since 1991, to have to play his way onto the team is pretty insulting.

Bernie says no thanks, and that's it. There's no goodbye, no Bernie Williams Day, just a beloved Yankee sent on his way. It's not my job to tell the Yankees how to run their business. But this is not the right way to treat Bernie, and I don't think it's the right baseball decision for the team. I am going to miss the guitar. I am going to miss No. 51 even more.

It's what makes the return of No. 46, Andy Pettitte, so welcome.

Andy left as a free agent after the 2003 loss to the Marlins in the World Series, signing with his hometown Houston Astros. Now, four years later, he's back, and the sight of him walking in the door brings joy to my heart. Andy is as good a teammate as you could ever find, a man who is totally forthright and fully accountable, even after his name is mentioned in a MLB report on the use of performance-enhancing drugs in baseball. Most guys in similar circumstances swear on the Bible they are clean, or release some generic apology through their agent. Andy faces it straight-on, admitting he made a mistake. It takes a ton of courage to do that. It makes me respect him even more.

Andy brings the same courage to the mound, a pitcher who repeatedly proves you can't scout heart. The 594th pick in the 1990 free-agent draft, taken in the 22nd round, Andy was a chubby kid out of Deer Park High School in Texas projected to do nothing. He doesn't blow people away with his arm. But he winds up with 275 big league victories, a total that includes nineteen postseason wins and some of the biggest games in Yankee history.

It's no fault of Andy's, because he pitches superbly, but when we fall to the Blue Jays in late May, we are in an unimaginable spot: last place. Our record is 21–29. Up and down the roster, guys are not playing to their usual level. We are so far behind the Red Sox—fourteen and a half games—that we're in danger of being lapped.

We head into Toronto, and, believe it or not, things get even messier. We have a 7–5 lead on the Blue Jays in the ninth inning when Jorge hits a pop fly to third. The Jays' Howie Clark camps under it. Alex is running with two out, and as he passes Clark he shouts, "Ha!" A startled Clark backs off the ball, thinking the shortstop had called for it, and it drops. We score three more runs and win, 10–5. Later, Blue Jays manager John Gibbons rips Alex for what he considers a bush-league play. Other Blue Jays chime in, too.

There is no doubt that Alex has a knack for winding up in the middle of things, but I also think that people come after him much harder because he is Alex Rodriguez. If Jorge or Derek had yelled at a fielder the way Alex did, I don't think it would have become nearly as big a deal. You know how many times hitters and base runners have pulled similar stunts to try to distract me? You know what I hear when I go to field a bunt?

"Third!" one guy yells.

"Second!" another guy yells.

People scream to get me flustered so I will throw to the wrong base. And what about when infielders pretend to be fielding a throw from an outfielder to trick a runner? Is that okay?

I get the save in the "Ha!" game and hope it's the start of a turnaround. It is my first save in almost a month, and only my fourth in a season that has had many more lowlights than highlights. Four weeks into the season, I have an ERA of 10-something. In the media, there is speculation that I have lost it, that my days as a dominant closer are done. The doubters do not include me, so I'm not worried. I know I will get sharper. The day I go out there feeling overmatched, I won't need anybody else to tell me it's time to hang it up.

The worst moment for me is probably a game at home against the Mariners when we start a rookie pitcher, Matt DeSalvo. Matt is just up from the minors and he delivers seven sparkling innings in his big league debut, giving up just three hits and one run to the Mariners. In the eighth, an ump blows a call when Willie Bloomquist tries to steal second, calling him safe even though Willie is out by the length of a fishing pole, and the Mariners tie the game. In the ninth, I blow the game when Adrian Beltre mashes a misplaced cutter—supposed to be up and in, but it is out over the plate—for a home run, and we lose. Blowing a save is never fun, but for me to shortchange young Matt DeSalvo, who spoke afterward about the "majesty" of the moment when he was about to throw his first big league pitch to Ichiro, really gets me. The poor kid has nothing to show for his phenomenal debut.

In the clubhouse afterward, I seek him out.

"You pitched a great game. I am sorry about the ending," I say.

"That's okay, Mo. It happens. I know you did your best," Matt says.

We head to Fenway for three games, and one of the tougher weekends Alex has probably ever had. Boston fans are having great fun with Alex's tabloid troubles, riding him unmercifully.

We split the first two games of the series and with the score tied with two out in the ninth on Sunday night, Alex rips an 0–2 pitch from Jonathan Papelbon into the Red Sox bullpen. He has never had a happier trip around the bases, I guarantee you that. It's the biggest hit of our season. I get the save. We take two out of three in Fenway. It is something to build on.

A few weeks later, the team has an inter-league series scheduled in Colorado against the Rockies. Our oldest son, Mariano Jr., is graduating from middle school. It is our first graduation as a family. I can't recall ever asking Mr. T for a favor before. I've definitely never asked out of a road trip.

"I know this is a lot to ask, but would you be okay if I didn't make the Colorado trip so I can attend my son's graduation? It means so much to me, and to our family," I say.

He looks surprised. He pauses. "Mo, I would love to accommodate you, but it would be really hard for me to do that. It sends the wrong message. It wouldn't be fair to let you do this and then not extend the same courtesy to others."

I hear him out, and I know that even asking this is putting him in an awkward spot. But for once, I am not my compliant, team-first self. I don't think Mr. T understands the significance of this to me. I dropped out of school when I was just a little older than my son. My father dropped out even earlier. This day is something that needs to be celebrated properly.

"I am sorry, but I am going to go whether I have permission or not. It's very important that I be there," I say.

"I can't stop you from going," Mr. T says, "but if it comes to the eighth or ninth inning and we have a lead and we need you and you're not there, what do I say to people? That you are gone without permission? I can't tell people I gave you permission when there are twenty-four other guys counting on you. I can't do that."

"Okay," I reply. I need to think about it. I leave his office and talk it over with Clara. I explain the conversation to her, and the more I reflect on it, the more I realize I cannot defy my manager. It's just not how I operate.

Next time I see Mr. T, I let him know I've reconsidered.

"I will be on the trip to Colorado," I say. "It wouldn't be right not to be with the team."

I explain to my son that I want to be at his graduation more than anything, but the Yankees won't give me permission to miss the trip. I tell him how much I love him and how proud I am of him.

Mariano Jr. is very understanding. The sad truth is that he, Jafet, and Jaziel are very accustomed to my absence at big occasions. Baseball has given our family a lot, but the schedule is unforgiving.

We get swept in Colorado and I don't even pitch.

By the All-Star break we have managed to get to .500, so we forget the first half of the season and remember how to play like the New York Yankees. In back-to-back games against the Rays, we outscore them, 38–9, pounding out forty-five hits. We go 24–8 after the break and pull within four games of the Red Sox. A big part of the surge is our new secret weapon in the bullpen, a powerful twenty-one-year-old from Nebraska named Joba Chamberlain. Joba throws 99-mile-per-hour fastballs, and his slider is his best pitch. In his first twelve games, he doesn't give up an earned run and strikes out more than a man per inning, pumping his fist after every punch-out. By the end of the regular season, he has thirty-four strikeouts in twenty-four innings, and an ERA of 0.38. Of the nineteen games in which he has pitched, we've won seventeen. It is something to behold.

We're in the playoffs for the thirteenth straight year, but for the first time in ten years, we are not the AL East champions. As the wild-card team, we open on the road against the Cleveland Indians. Johnny Damon drives a CC Sabathia pitch over the fence to start the game, and then Chien-Ming Wang takes the mound, a steady sinkerballer who won nineteen games for us in each of the last two years.

There is no reason not to have a ton of faith in Wang. He has won six of his last seven starts and handled the playoff pressure well.

But Wang is wild. In the first inning, he walks two, hits one, and gives up three singles and three runs. His sinkerball isn't sinking; it's flying all over the park. By the time he leaves in the fifth, his line is nine hits and eight runs. Even though Sabathia doesn't have his best stuff, either, we lose, 12–3.

Game 2 is now a must-win and, fortunately, we have Andy Pettitte on the mound. He needs to go deep in the game, hand the ball to Joba, who will hand the ball to me. Andy proves yet again that his competitive makeup ranks with anybody's. He has runners on in every inning and gets out of the jam every time. In the sixth, Grady Sizemore hits a leadoff triple, and has a great view of Andy getting Asdrúbal Cabrera on a bouncer back to the mound, followed by strikeouts of Travis Hafner and Víctor Martínez.

The game moves to the seventh, the only

run coming on Melky Cabrera's homer off Indians starter Roberto Hernández in the third. With one out in the bottom of the seventh, Jhonny Peralta doubles and Kenny Lofton walks. Mr. T signals for Joba, who makes his postseason debut by striking out Franklin Gutiérrez and getting Casey Blake to fly to right.

It's still 1–0 at the top of the eighth. But as Joba comes set to face Sizemore, he begins swatting and waving his arms around on the mound. It is not a stray mosquito or two. It is a swarm of bugs called midges, and in the heat of an unseasonably warm fall night— eighty-one degrees at game time—they are descending on Joba and his sweat-soaked neck and face by the hundreds, if not thousands. They cover his neck. They are in his ears. Flying around his mouth and nose and eyes. He keeps flailing and it does no good. Neither does the insect spray Gene Monahan brings out.

The bullpen is completely midge-free. I am

not bothered once. But seeing Joba's reaction, I can't believe the umpires aren't stopping the game. They stop it for a torrential rainstorm. Why not for a torrential bug storm? Maybe because the midges aren't nearly as bad by the dugout, Mr. T doesn't fully grasp what Joba is going through, and doesn't push the umps to halt play. So it continues, and for the first time since he got to the majors two months before, Joba Chamberlain, strike machine, turns into a wild, sputtering mess. He walks Sizemore on four pitches—a first in his big league career. He wild-pitches him to second, and two batters later, he wild-pitches him home to tie the game. The poor kid is trying to keep his composure, but with the midges continuing to attack, he hits one guy and walks another, before finally getting Peralta on a slider away to end the inning.

Joba leaves the game. And the midges leave the field as mysteriously as they came.

We have a man on second in the top of the ninth, but Alex strikes out. I get the Indians in order and we go to extra innings. After I get through a bumpy tenth—I strike out Peralta with the bases loaded—we do nothing in the top of the eleventh, our offense having produced just two singles since the fourth.

When Hafner lines a single with the bases loaded off Luis Vizcaíno, the Indians have a 2–1 victory, and we have another serious hole to escape from.

Back in the midge-free Bronx, Mr. T starts Roger Clemens, forty-four years old and lured out of retirement to help stabilize our rotation. He has battled injuries and inconsistency, and tonight is no different.

Phil Hughes is stellar in relief, Damon and Canó sock big hits, and I save an 8–4 victory. We need one more to take the series back to Cleveland for a fifth game. It's Wang's turn again, and, pitching on just three days' rest, the Indians smack him around. We fall behind, 6–1, and though Alex and Abreu homer, it's another game where we don't pitch, or hit, well enough to win.

Our season ends with a 6–4 loss.

When I go into the off-season, I am like a fisherman going out to sea. I'll be gone awhile, and I don't look back. I don't think about baseball. As much as I love the game, if I am not playing in the World Series, I don't watch the World Series. It is no different this year, when the Red Sox are playing the Rockies.

By the time I turn thirty-eight in November, I am in Panama for the funeral of my friend Chico Heron, who has passed away after a long illness. I've known Chico for most of my life, and I loved him. If he hadn't scouted me, I never would have made the big leagues. If he hadn't believed in me, I don't know where I would be.

Chico was the biggest asset Panamanian

baseball players ever had. You could be playing on a rock-ribbed sandlot that was miles from everywhere, and you'd look up and Chico would be there. Then you'd be at the biggest stadium in Panama City, and he'd be there, too. He loved baseball, loved the hunt for diamonds in the rough, and loved helping those guys shine. Chico didn't worry that I was skin and bones and only throwing in the mid-eighties. He saw potential. He saw what I might become—a kid who, with more weight and a lot of work, might be a legitimate prospect. He recommended me to his boss, Herb Raybourn, and soon enough I was on my way to Tampa.

Even more than his eye for talent, though, Chico had goodness in his soul. He knew the right way to do things. Over and over, he would talk to me about giving everything I had at all times, about being respectful and keeping my focus and persevering through the tough times that are definitely a part of the game and of life.

"Trust yourself and believe in yourself," Chico would tell me. "When you have that trust, and you are willing to work, there's no telling what you can accomplish."

I listened, and it changed my life.

NOTES FROM MO

A Save Opportunity

Everybody knows what a win is, but a "save" is a statistic that Major League Baseball first officially began keeping track of in 1969. (The year I was born! I am sure there is no connection between the two.)

In order for a relief pitcher to earn a save his team must win the game and he must be on the mound when they do. The team can also have no more than a three-run lead when the pitcher enters the game. In other words, if the Yankees are winning 10–0 and I get three outs in the ninth, the team gets a win, but that does not count as a save.

Closing Time

It's a time of big transition in my baseball life. Mr. T is gone, and Mr. G—Joe Girardi— is here. He's the third manager of my major league career, and the first, of course, who has been not just a teammate but a catcher of mine. The first time we were a battery in a real game was against the Rangers in 1996. I struck out Rusty Greer and sailed through two quick innings with Joe. He was upbeat and high-energy, a small guy with a big presence

who was good at blocking pitches and calling games. A team-oriented player. Batting
eighth, right ahead of Derek, he had the most
sacrifice bunts on the squad that year, stole
thirteen bases, and had one of the biggest hits
of the World Series—the run-scoring triple
off of Greg Maddux in the decisive Game 6.

Having a new manager is a big change, but
Joe is as easy to play for as he was to play with.
He tells me he wants to limit me to one inning
whenever possible, and be judicious when it's
my turn to pitch.

Whether it's the new manager or my new
catcher, José Molina—Jorge misses much of
the season with an injury, so the Yankees get a
Molina brother to fill in—I begin the year as
if I'm about to turn twenty-nine, not thirty-
nine. Two months into the season, I have
twenty-six strikeouts, two walks, an ERA of
0.38, and fifteen saves. We go on a seven-game
winning streak after that, and I get my nine-
teenth save by striking out the side against
the Padres. It would feel a whole lot better if

316

we weren't just five games over .500 (50–45) when the All-Star Game arrives at the original Yankee Stadium for the final time.

It's my ninth All-Star Game, and with our new stadium being built next door, it's baseball's way of saying farewell to the House That Ruth Built, the most famous baseball stadium in the world. The most powerful part for me is seeing George Steinbrenner, whose health is failing. He hasn't been around all year and you can't mistake how much it means to him to be here. When he rides in from the outfield in a golf cart before the game, Mr. George is weeping. He hands baseballs to four Yankee Hall of Famers—Whitey Ford, Yogi Berra, Goose Gossage, and Reggie Jackson. They embrace him—then throw the balls to their ceremonial catchers: Whitey to Derek; Yogi to Joe Girardi; Reggie to Alex; Goose to me.

I don't remember when I first officially met Mr. George, but I was already in the big leagues. If he was around spring training when I was younger, I watched him from afar, but went about my work.

Mr. George is surrounded by his family at the All-Star Game, and he looks overcome by the festivities. It's sad because Mr. George has always been such a commanding (and demanding) presence. I wish I could thank him for giving me the honor of wearing the uniform of the New York Yankees, but I am not sure whether to approach him. I decide it's best to let him enjoy his family and the farewell to the Stadium, a place he has helped make one of the most legendary venues in sports.

It is one of the last times I ever see Mr. George Steinbrenner.

We win eight in a row to start the second half. Joba, now a starter, pitches a 1–0 masterpiece at Fenway in late July, and I finish it with back-to-back strikeouts. That puts us just three games out of first—the closest we've been since the first week of May.

And then we slide back to mediocrity again. We lose four of five games and give up forty-four runs in the process, not the sort of pitching that's going to take you places. We lost Wang in June to an ankle injury, and we have only one starter—Mussina—with an ERA under 4.00. Offensively, we're just an average team this year. Not a winning combination.

The Red Sox come to town in late August, and it's a series we really need to win, if not sweep. We do neither. Andy gets roughed up in the opener, a 7–3 defeat, and in the next game we send out Sidney Ponson, but the Red Sox's Dustin Pedroia puts on a show, getting three hits, scoring four runs, and driving in four with a grand slam off David Robertson. He's covered with dirt from cap to cleat, and plays like it's the last game he'll ever get to play.

Until he comes back the next day, and the day after, and plays the same way.

There are a lot of players I admire, and Pedroia is at the top of the list. It's a special thing to see, a little guy who does whatever it takes. I've seen many top-notch second basemen in the big leagues. Roberto Alomar could beat you with his glove, his legs, or his bat. Robinson Canó has a beautiful swing and is as good in the field as almost anybody. Chuck Knoblauch was another guy who could take over a game with his speed and grit. But if you are looking for a guy who's going to go full out and do whatever it takes to win, Dustin Pedroia has to be right there with anybody.

Three weeks later, our season is effectively over, and so is our postseason streak of thirteen years. The Rays are the AL East champions, the Red Sox win the wild-card. The Yankees finish six games back at 89–73. Like Derek and Jorge, I've been to the playoffs every year of my career, but the simple truth is that we don't deserve to go this year. I finish with one of the best statistical years of my career (39 saves in 40 chances, 1.40 ERA, 77 strikeouts, and 6 walks), but all of that and 45 cents will get me on the bus to Chorrera.

Our final piece of business in the 2008 season is to complete our goodbye to Yankee Stadium. After 85 years and 26 world championships, the final game is played on September 21, against the Orioles. The gates open seven hours early so fans can walk around and have a proper farewell.

I think about the first time I stood on the mound here in the postseason—top of the twelfth inning in the 1995 ALDS against the Mariners, striking out Jay Buhner to begin three and one-third innings of relief, before Jim Leyritz belted his homer in the bottom of the fifteenth.

I remember celebrating the sweep of the Braves four years later with Jorge and Tino and everybody, and I remember kneeling in prayer on the mound as Aaron Boone rounded the bases four years after that.

These are just a few special memories of a Panamanian boy who was going to be a mechanic. What about all the other historic moments, and all the superstars who called this Stadium their home, from Ruth to Gehrig to DiMaggio to Berra to Mantle and now to Jeter?

Derek says the history and tradition is just going to move across the street, but can the spirit of this Stadium really be recaptured? I don't know.

Yankee Stadium is not just a home office for triumph. It is where I grow up as a pitcher, and as a man, a place with special, spiritual retreats deep within it. There is the trainer's room, where I spend all those middle innings with Geno, a young man and an older man bonding over a mutual belief in the importance of thoroughness and hard work.

There is the tunnel beneath the left-field stands, where I make the walk to the bullpen, turning left out of the clubhouse and following the corridor around, behind home plate, and continuing down toward the left-field foul pole, where I turn right and wind through Monument Park toward the pen.

There is the bullpen bench, where I watch the game, taking in the rich green field before me. I love that bench, and how I mark the rhythms of my job there, playful and silly at first, then turning more serious as I wait for the phone to ring, and my world becomes centered on getting outs, and a victory.

I love that bench. I love it so much that the Yankees let me take it home when the old Stadium closed for good.

And then there is the bullpen mound, where I go to work after I get the call, going through my precise warm-up routine and waiting for the doors to open, to make my solitary run toward the mound.

I cherish this place. I want to be the last man to stand on that mound. I want to throw the last pitch, and get the last out.

The power and emotion of the day never

let up. It seems as though half of Cooperstown is on the field before the game. Yankee greats are everywhere. Bernie is there, of course, and he probably gets the biggest roar of all. Julia Ruth Stevens, the Babe's ninety-two-year-old daughter, throws the first pitch to Jorge. Yogi Berra is talking about how the place will always be in his heart, wearing the heavy wool flannels that players of his day wore, before uniform manufacturers came up with lighter, cooler fabrics.

Julia's father homered in the first game ever played in the Stadium, and the homers continue. In the bottom of the third, Johnny Damon rips a three-run blast that gives the Yankees an early lead, but the Orioles tie it up in the top of the fourth. Then José Molina, who has had two homers all season, hits his third into left center, putting us back on top, 5–3.

I make my way down the left-field corridor beneath the stands in the sixth. I don't want to leave this place. I don't want this to be the last time.

Nostalgia doesn't hit me very often. It's hitting me now like a freight train.

For the last time, I am in the pen, my baseball home for fourteen years.

The phone rings in the eighth. Mike Harkey answers.

"Mo, you got the ninth," Harkey says.

The bottom of the eighth ends with a ground out, and it's time.

The blue doors open.

"Enter Sandman" starts.

I make my last run across the outfield in the House That Ruth Built. The crowd is standing and cheering. It is surreal.

I get to the mound and pick up the ball. I need for this to be business as usual; I need to focus on these three outs, even if it is not business as usual at all.

The first Orioles batter is Jay Payton. He hit a three-run homer off me in Game 2 of the Subway Series eight years before, in case you have forgotten. Believe me, I have not.

I get Payton on a grounder to short, ably

handled by Derek. I get ahead on the next batter, 0–2, come with a hard cutter inside, and he bounces it to second. Two outs. One to go. But before I can throw another pitch, I see Wilson Betemit running from the dugout toward short. Joe wants Derek to leave the old place in a fitting way, with one last massive ovation. That is exactly what happens.

Derek Jeter, the last Yankee icon in a fabled Stadium, runs to the dugout accompanied by thunderous applause.

The next Orioles hitter is Brian Roberts. He has always been a tough out for me. On a 2–1 pitch, he hits a grounder to Cody Ransom at first. I break off the mound, but Cody takes it himself for the final out. He tucks the ball in my glove and shakes my hand. The Yankees didn't win enough games this year, but we won the last one ever played at 161st Street and River Avenue, and for that I am very grateful.

I know exactly what I am going to do with this ball. I am going to give it to George Steinbrenner. He is the one who deserves to have it.

Notes from Mo

Replacing a Legend

The original Yankee Stadium was already fifty years old when it closed in 1973 for two years to undergo a major renovation. But thirty years later, the Stadium needed more than just a massive facelift, and after years of negotiating with the city of New York, construction of a replacement got under way in August 2006. We could measure its progress every time we played a home game for the next two years—the new Stadium went up right across the street, on the site of a city park.

As a way of honoring Yankee history, the new Stadium was designed to include elements from the original building. But unlike the old place, two-thirds of the new Stadium's seating is in the lower bowl, unlike the stacked, three-tier design of the original. The new Yankee Stadium has 4,000 fewer seats overall (but each seat is a little wider), and triple the number of luxury boxes.

The price tag was a little higher for our new home, too. The original Yankee Stadium cost $2.5 million, which made it the most expensive sports stadium ever constructed at the time it opened. The new Yankee Stadium cost $1.5 *billion*.

During construction of the new Stadium, a construction worker who was secretly a big fan of the Boston Red Sox buried a David Ortiz jersey underneath the visitors' dugout, hoping to place a "hex" on the Yankees, much like the "Curse of the Bambino." But he bragged about it and the Yankees found out, forcing him to help them locate and remove the jersey. Later, the same worker said he had planted a 2004 ALCS scorecard somewhere in the Stadium, but he wouldn't reveal the location.

It's okay. I don't believe in curses, do you?

New Digs, Old Feelings

The early verdict on the new Yankee
Stadium is that batters are going to like it a lot
more than pitchers are. Home runs are flying
out of the place. Visiting teams might find it
a bit friendlier, too. For all its grandeur and
state-of-the-art features, the new park doesn't
hold noise, or home-team fervor, anywhere
near the way the old place did. It's an adjust-
ment when you are used to having a full-
throated full house. The old Stadium was our

tenth man—a loud and frenzied cauldron of pinstripe passion, with lots of lifelong fans in the stands. It's hard at first to see how the new place can duplicate that.

Some things are unaffected by new construction, though, and one of them is Derek's swing. In the eighth inning of game two in our new home, with the score tied 5–5 against the Indians, Derek swats a 3–1 pitch to right. He's off and running until the ball clears the fence.

Now it's on me. After a long fly to center, I give up two singles, before striking out Grady Sizemore. Mark DeRosa comes up. The count goes full and the runners are on the move. I throw the cutter away, hoping to nick the outside corner upstairs. As I wind and deliver, it's right where I want it. DeRosa thinks it is breaking outside and takes it, the umpire rings him up, and I have my first save in our new house.

The Yankees have dug deep to have a shiny new team for the brand-new ballpark, spending tens of millions to bring in CC Sabathia, A. J. Burnett, and Mark Teixeira, but it doesn't stop us from getting off to another sluggish start, including a forgettable weekend in Fenway in late April. We get swept, and the most painful loss comes Friday night. I strike out Ortiz and Pedroia and am one out from saving a 4–2 victory for Joba when I leave a 1–0 cutter over the heart of the plate to Jason Bay, who hits it halfway to Boston Harbor. It's another muffed save against a team that has gotten to me more than any other by far. I think it comes down to familiarity. I have pitched against them so many times, their hitters have a much keener sense of how and when my ball moves.

We wind up losing in eleven on a Kevin Youkilis walkoff, and lose Saturday when Burnett can't hold a six-run lead. The Sox win again Sunday when Jacoby Ellsbury steals home off Andy. A couple of weeks later, I give up back-to-back homers to Carl Crawford and Evan Longoria of the Rays, the first time

I've ever done that in my career. I've already given up more homers than I did all of the previous year. I had minor shoulder surgery in October and I am still not where I want to be velocity-wise. I know that my arm is going to get stronger but there's less margin for error than when I was throwing 96 or 97 miles per hour. Regaining my command is critical.

With the exception of our results against the Red Sox—we lose eight straight to them to start the season—I see something in this club that I haven't seen in a long time. We are fighting to the end, game in and game out. Teams always say they do that, but not that many really do.

Example? Early in June at the Stadium, I have a brutal outing against the Rays, giving up three earned runs in two-thirds of an inning.

The next day? We score three times in the bottom of the eighth and I pitch a clean ninth, and we move into first place with the win. It's the twentieth come-from-behind victory for us and the season is barely two months old. We keep the comeback theme going in a Subway Series with the Mets, thanks to the all-out hustle of Mark Teixeira.

We are trailing, down to our last out, after I give up an RBI double to David Wright in the eighth. Derek, who singled, is on second, and Teixeira, who was intentionally walked, is on first. Alex is at the plate. Frankie Rodríguez, the Mets closer, fires and gets Alex to hit a high, but weak, pop-up. Alex slams the bat down, because he had a fastball to hit and missed it. The ball floats into short right behind second baseman Luis Castillo. It is way up there. Castillo settles under it but somehow it glances off his glove. Derek is running hard, of course, and Teixeira is right behind him, busting it from the moment Alex makes contact. Mark scores and we win, not just on an error you might see once every five years but on the hustle of a star player who goes hard until the game is over.

That's what winners do.

Three games out of first, with a 51–37 record at the All-Star break, we go on our best roll of the season. We win eighteen of our first twenty-three games after the break, including a four-game sweep of the Red Sox. We blow right past them into first place.

The last of those games is a microcosm of our season. Down 2–1 going into the bottom of the eighth, Damon and Teixeira blast back-to-back homers, and Jorge follows with a two-run single. I close it by getting Ellsbury to ground out. I go seven weeks and twenty-one appearances without giving up a run, and by the time we pull off another four-game sweep, this time of the Rays, we are forty-one games over .500 (91–50) with a nine-game lead. I am pretty darn sure this is not going to be another year when we have a division series meltdown.

I have thirty-nine saves, and my ERA is 1.72. By mid-September, I have converted thirty-six consecutive save opportunities.

The sportswriters have stopped predicting my retirement.

Then, on a Friday night in Seattle, I come on in the ninth with a 1–0 lead to save a game for A. J. Burnett, who outpitched the great Félix Hernández. I strike out the first two batters looking and then Mike Sweeney hits a long double. The next hitter is Ichiro. He is so good at going the other way that I want to come inside hard to jam him. I deliver a cutter, but the ball stays over the plate. Ichiro smashes it over the right-field fence, a stunning turnaround in the space of two pitches. Against a hitter that good, you have to be better. I miss my spot. Save blown. Game over.

"I'm sorry," I tell A. J. "You deserved to win that game."

"Don't worry about it, Mo. You've saved plenty for me," A. J. says. I walk out of the clubhouse with a chocolate ice-cream cone but even the sweetness does not take away the sting of letting down the team.

We draw the Twins in the division series and coast to a Game 1 victory at the Stadium behind CC Sabathia.

Game 2 is much tenser. The Twins rally to take a 3–1 lead into the bottom of the ninth, with Joe Nathan, one of the best closers in the league, on for the save. Nathan has saved forty-seven games during the regular year, but before he can record an out, Mark Teixeira singles to right and Alex deposits a pitch in the bullpen to tie the game at 3–3. It's the first magical October moment in the new ballpark, and it's followed by another in the eleventh, when Mark hits a walk-off home run. We lead two games to none.

We head to Minneapolis and take a 2–1 lead thanks in part to another Rodriguez home run, and a tremendous defensive play by Derek and Jorge. Nick Punto doubles to lead off the eighth, then Denard Span singles up the middle. Derek snares it before it reaches the outfield but knows he can't throw out the speedy Span. Punto, however, has rounded third aggressively, thinking about scoring. Derek fires to Jorge, who rifles a throw to Alex, whose swipe tag catches Punto trying to slide back into third. It's a colossal baserunning blunder, but only perfect execution gets us the out.

I am warming up in the bullpen. You can almost feel the air come out of the Metrodome.

One batter later, I come in to face Joe Mauer, with the tying run on base. Mauer is a .365 hitter that year, the AL MVP, but you can't worry about that. You trust your stuff and know that if you throw your best pitch, you can get anybody out, even Mauer. My pitch busts Mauer's bat as he grounds out to first. We sweep.

Now it's on to meet the Angels in our first ALCS since 2004. We take Game 1 behind CC, 4–1, and then Alex drills a fastball over the right-field wall in the eleventh inning of

Game 2, to even the score. It's Alex's third game-tying homer of the postseason, and we win two innings later when Jerry Hairston singles, gets bunted to second, and scores on a wild throw. Back in Anaheim, the Angels win in extra innings, but CC pitches another great game in a Game 4 blowout. We head home to close out the Angels in six games, Andy winning, me saving my third game of the series.

Next up: the Philadelphia Phillies, baseball's defending World Series champions.

Being in the World Series doesn't seem as if it comes with the uniform anymore—not with six years having passed since our previous appearance. I have a new appreciation for how hard it is to get here. I am a month away from turning forty. I don't know if I will pass this way again.

My first big test comes against Chase Utley, with two on and one out in the top of the eighth in Game 2. Cliff Lee was dominant in Game 1 with a complete-game 6–1 victory. Utley belted two homers in support of him.

Now here Utley is again. Burnett delivers a superb effort, besting Pedro Martínez, whom the Phillies acquired just for games like this. He pitches well, but Teixeira and Matsui get him with solo homers, and Jorge has a huge pinch single. I am protecting a 3–1 lead as Utley works the count full. I go at him with nothing but cutters, mostly working on the outside, for good reason. He tries to pull everything. I don't know if this is another instance of a lefty hitter aiming for the short porch in left field, but Utley sure seems to be leaning that way. On a 3–2 pitch, I come at him with another cutter away. He makes solid contact but hits a bouncer that goes from Canó to Jeter to Teixeira for an inning-ending double play.

An inning later, I get Matt Stairs swinging to finish things up, and we square the Series at one.

With Alex, Matsui, and Nick Swisher homering in Game 3, and Andy pitching around two Jayson Werth homers, we take an 8–5 decision in Citizens Bank, and then score three in the ninth to break a 4–4 tie in Game 4, the big hits coming from Alex and Jorge. I nail down a 7–4 victory with a 1-2-3 ninth. We are one game away.

The Phillies have other ideas, pushing the Series to a sixth game by winning their last game of the year in Citizens Bank. We return to the Bronx for Game 6, Andy vs. Pedro. Matsui hits a two-run homer in the bottom of the second to get us going, then a two-run single in the third, and a two-run double in the fifth. He has six RBIs in three at-bats.

If only this guy could hit in the clutch.

A two-run Ryan Howard homer makes the score 7–3, but Joba and Dámaso Marte shut them down from there, and I get the final two outs in the eighth and then two more in the ninth, sandwiched around a Carlos Ruiz walk. Shane Victorino steps in. The Stadium crowd is on its feet. Victorino battles. He always battles. He's another one of those guys, like Pedroia, who can play on my team anytime. He falls behind, 1–2, then fouls off four straight pitches. Finally, he works the count full.

Utley, Howard, and Werth are the next three hitters. I need to get Victorino right now. I throw one more cut fastball, down, and Victorino pounds it into the ground, a harmless bouncer to Robby Canó, who tosses to Mark for the out. I pump my fist before the ball is even in his glove. I turn toward the infield and keep running, and now it feels as if the whole team is chasing me.

I am laughing like a little kid playing keep-away. This is the fourth time I've gotten the final out in the World Series, and, maybe because it has been so long, it feels like the best one of all. It's beautiful not just that we won but how we won. Hideki Matsui, a total pro, hits .615 and knocks in eight runs in six games. Dámaso Marte retires the last twelve hitters he faces, among them Utley and Howard, both of whom he strikes out in the final game. Andy pitches his second clincher, on three days' rest. Derek hits .407 and Damon hits .364. Alex, a new man this October, has six RBIs; Jorge, five.

What is also beautiful is that for the first time, Clara and the boys are at every game, and so are my parents and in-laws. We share the whole experience together. What could be better than to celebrate a big victory, surrounded by the people you love the most?

24

No. 42

You know I love my uniform. I also love my number—No. 42. The most famous No. 42, Jackie Robinson, was a third baseman with the Brooklyn Dodgers who broke baseball's "color barrier" in 1947, becoming the first player of African American heritage to play major league baseball.

I wish I could have met Jackie Robinson. I wish I could have shaken his hand and thanked him for what he did not only for baseball, but for players like me, whose skin is brown or black or some color in between. But Jackie died a young man at age fifty-three, in 1972. I was three years old at the time, feeding chips into Mr. Big Mouth.

Before I report for my twenty-first season of professional baseball, however, I get to meet Jackie's widow, Rachel Robinson. She is regal and gracious, intelligent and tireless—a champion of freedom and equality. I am not in awe of too many people, but I am in awe of Rachel Robinson. More than forty years after she lost her husband, Rachel continues to keep his legacy alive. We meet at a fund-raising event in Manhattan for the Jackie Robinson Foundation. I am there with Hank Aaron— I know who he is now—speaking about the privilege and pressure of being the last player to wear Jackie's 42.

The privilege part couldn't be more obvious; who wouldn't want to share a uniform number with the great Jackie Robinson? The pressure is living up to a man who changed the world, conducting himself with dignity every step of the way.

I don't know if any person can match that standard. I am no pioneer, I can tell you that. Roberto Clemente was the first Latin star, and many others, including Vic Power and Orlando Cepeda, followed. Humberto Robinson, a relief pitcher, was the first big league player from Panama. I am a simple man who measures his impact in a smaller way: by treating people and playing the game the right way.

Our home opener is always a festive occasion, especially when it begins with a ceremony to hand out our World Series rings. But there is a dark cloud hovering over this year's party. A month before spring training starts, I learn that Geno Monahan has been diagnosed with cancer. As trainer, he has spent four decades caring for Yankee ballplayers. Now he has to take care of himself. He takes a leave from the team to undergo chemotherapy but arranges to be at the Stadium for opening day. He is introduced right after Joe Girardi. Jorge asks the emcee to wait before he introduces anyone else. The crowd stands to cheer for Geno, and the Yankee players who owe him so much, move to the dugout railing, cheering for him, too. Geno is choking up, tapping his heart. I am choking up, too.

Geno wants to rejoin us by early June. I pray he finds the strength he needs to get through this and back to the job he loves.

We celebrate our rings and Geno with a victory that day, even if a former teammate, Bobby Abreu, gives us a scare when he hits a grand slam off of David Robertson in the top of the ninth to make the score 7–5. Joe calls for me to get the last two outs. I strike out Torii Hunter and up steps... Hideki Matsui, World Series hero, who signed with the Angels, our opening day opponent, during the off-season. A few hours earlier, I clapped when he got his ring, now I want to put him away so people will clap for us. It's weird stuff sometimes, this free-agency racket, but when I look in at Jorge's glove, Godzilla himself could be in the batter's box and I wouldn't be ruffled.

Hideki pops up my first pitch to second, and the game is over.

Geno actually returns ahead of schedule, and maybe it's the inspiration of a sixty-five-year-old trainer that makes me feel almost young. We have the best record in the majors (44–27) as we take the field in Phoenix against the Diamondbacks. We have to rally to tie in the ninth but go ahead in the tenth when Curtis Granderson, our new center fielder, smokes a homer into the stands. I come out for the tenth looking to nail down a victory. I have retired twenty-four straight hitters, a streak that ends when Stephen Drew singles to right and Justin Upton cracks a double. Joe orders me to walk the cleanup man, Miguel Montero, to set up the force at home.

So the bases are loaded with Diamondbacks, and everybody is wondering if I am having flashbacks to the 2001 World Series.

I give them the answer:

No.

That was November 4, 2001. This is June 23, 2010.

I had hair then. I have no hair now.

I had Scott Brosius and Tino Martinez on the corners then. I have Alex Rodriguez and Mark Teixeira on the corners now.

I was thirty-one then. I am forty now.

I don't carry things that do me no good. I let them go, so I can be light.

The batter is Chris Young, the center fielder. I bust him inside and he pops up to Francisco Cervelli, my catcher. Next up is Adam LaRoche. He has all five RBIs in the game for the Diamondbacks. I run a cutter in on his hands and he pops out to Alex.

Now the hitter is Mark Reynolds. He leads

the team in homers. Not a guy you want to miss your spot with.

I get strike one on a cutter away that Reynolds looks at. I miss away, then hit the outside corner with another cutter. On the 2–2 pitch, I want to go up the ladder—change his eye level. I fire another cutter, up. Reynolds whiffs.

Game over.

Two days later, we are in Los Angeles to face the Dodgers, our first game ever against Mr. T. I give him a big hug before the game. He is not just the man who led us to four world championships; he's the man who saw something in me that made him willing to give me a chance to become the Yankees' closer. You never forget that.

"Take it easy on us tonight, okay, Mo?" he says. "These guys have never seen a cutter like yours before."

I laugh and am on my way. CC Sabathia pitches four-hit, one-run ball through eight, and I take the ball for the ninth, three outs away from saving a 2–1 victory.

Due up are Manny Ramírez, Matt Kemp, and James Loney. I strike out all three. I make sure not to look into the Dodger dugout for a reaction.

While we're in town, my old bullpen buddy Mike Borzello, who came to the Dodgers with Mr. T, asks if I'd be willing to talk to Jonathan Broxton, the Dodgers' closer. He's a kid the size of a boxcar, a young man with a great arm who has a strong start to the year but is suffering from some confidence issues. I introduce myself during batting practice and ask him how things are going.

"I'm just not doing the job the way I did last year," he says. Broxton talks about how confident and in control he felt when he was blowing away the league the year before. I can tell he is tying himself in knots trying to figure out what he is doing wrong.

"This is going to sound boring and obvious," I say, "but you know what I think about when I come into a save situation? I think about getting three outs as fast as I can. Don't worry about getting beat. It's going to happen. It happens to everybody. These are major league hitters and they're going to get you sometimes. The best thing a closer can have is a short memory. You can't take what happened yesterday out to the mound today. If you do that, you have no shot at succeeding."

In the series finale, Clayton Kershaw holds us to two runs on four hits. Broxton comes in to close it. I like the kid and wish him well, just not right now. He strikes out Teixeira. I'm thinking maybe I should have talked to him after the series, but then Alex singles, Robby doubles, and Jorge singles. Curtis walks. Chad Huffman singles, and we score four times to tie the game at six, smacking Broxton with as rough a blown save as he will have all year. We win it an inning later when Robby hits a two-run homer in the tenth.

"Thanks for talking to Brox," Mr. T says, next time I see him. "Whatever you said, he got a whole lot worse."

We go into the All-Star break in first place, with a record of 56–32, and even though I am selected to the team for the eleventh time, I sit it out to rest a cranky knee. The game is played in Anaheim. The date is July 13, and it includes prayers and a tearful goodbye: Mr. George Steinbrenner dies that morning in a Tampa hospital, nine days after his eightieth birthday. It is just two days since the death of Bob Sheppard, the Yankees' legendary announcer. Death and illness are part of life, of course, but that does not make it any easier to lose these men who brought so much to the Yankees and to baseball.

It's hard to know why anything happens in life, or why we seem capable of terrorizing the Minnesota Twins on command. We sweep them again in the postseason this year, making it nine straight October victories against them, and twelve out of the last fourteen. We have eliminated them in division series play four times in eight years and always seem to do it by coming from behind, as we do in two of our three victories this year, including Game 1.

I have more success against the Twins than against any other team. My career ERA in the Metrodome and at Target Field is 1.09 and overall against the Twins, it's 1.24. I can't explain it. I blew a save against them earlier this year at Yankee Stadium, allowing a grand slam to Jason Kubel, but otherwise have gone through them like a machete in a cornfield, especially in the playoffs; I have pitched sixteen and two-thirds innings against the Twins in the postseason and have given up no runs. The funny thing is that most of their big guns have hit me pretty well. Joe Mauer hits .286 against me. Justin Morneau and Michael Cuddyer hit .250 off me. It's not as if I have some master game plan against this club. I just always seem to get the outs I need. I have confidence against this team.

I take that confidence with me into Game 1 of the ALCS against the Rangers in Arlington. Michael Young is at the plate, with one out in the bottom of the ninth, the tying run on second. We have climbed out of a massive hole, taking a 6–5 lead on a homer from Robby in the seventh and a five-run outburst in the eighth. These two innings have left Rangers president Nolan Ryan with a pained look on his face, as if he'd eaten something sour.

Young is a tough out, a career .320 hitter against me. I don't fear any hitter, but I respect some more than others, and Michael Young has earned my respect. Jorge and I know we need to move the ball around and keep him guessing. I start with a cutter up and a cutter in, and he fouls off both. I barely miss with two more cutters, one in, one away. I am positive the 1–2 pitch is a strike—knee-high on the outside corner—but I don't get the call. I take the ball back from Jorge. I'm not going to start staring down umpires or showing them up now.

I have a pitch to make.

I come in with a two-seamer that is in and higher than I want, probably the best pitch to hit of the at-bat; Young fouls it off. Now Jorge sets up outside. He wants it up. I throw a nasty cutter right to his glove.

Young swings through it. Getting him has everything to do with working both sides of the plate, and then hitting that last spot. Some outs are more gratifying than others. This is a very good out.

One pitch later, I get Josh Hamilton in on the fists and he bouncers a slow grounder to third for the final out, and a stirring comeback victory. But being three victories away from returning to the Series doesn't mean anything, because we don't come close to getting them. Almost every battle for the rest of the ALCS is won by the Rangers, who outpitch us, outhit us, and outplay us. They also outscore us, 38–19, winning in six games. After Hamilton hits four homers and seven RBIs in six games, we give him the Barry Bonds treatment and intentionally walk him three times in one game. He is named the ALCS Most Valuable Player, and deservedly so.

Some things change: In the World Series, Hamilton's bat goes cold and the Rangers lose in five games to the Giants.

But some things don't.

I don't watch.

I turn forty-one a month after our season ends and am well into my off-season routine, which includes lots of fitness work and very little throwing, just enough playing catch to keep my arm loose. I make few concessions to age. I eat properly and take care of my body, so I don't think it's a miracle that I am still doing what I am doing. I listen to my body and give it what it needs.

If there is one thing I have changed, though, it is being more economical about everything. Who knows how many rocks I have left to throw? If I can get a batter out with one or two pitches, why throw three or four? I throw 928 pitches in 2010, over 60 innings. They are both the lowest totals of any full season of my career, and for a reason: There is no reason to stress myself unnecessarily.

In 2010, I threw seven innings in spring training and was ready to go. This year, I might not even throw that many. In my first game since I pitched in Game 6 against the Rangers, I face three Twins in the middle of March and strike them all out. One of them is Jason Kubel, who hit that grand slam the last time he faced me. This time he is caught looking at a 92-mile-per-hour fastball. It doesn't take me long to get loose for a game, and it doesn't take me long to get ready for the season. I don't aim to be low-maintenance; I aim to be no-maintenance. My mechanics are simple, and, as with any machine, the fewer moving parts, the less that can go wrong.

On opening day of the 2011 season, I throw twelve pitches to three Detroit Tigers to save a victory for Joba. It's an exhilarating way to start, but it still comes with mixed feelings, because my catcher is not Jorge Posada.

Nothing against Russell Martin, our new catcher, but when you grow up with a guy, eat all those meals at the Applebee's in Columbus with a guy, and share five World Series championships with a guy, you have a unique connection. Jorge has caught more of my pitches than anyone. That he's not doing it anymore is sad for him, but sad for me, too.

Apart from being a tremendous player and teammate, he is like a brother to me, the two of us connected by a shared mission: Get outs and win games.

I go about my job with a calculated calm; he goes about his with a passion that spews like lava from a volcano. We complement each other perfectly.

Jorge is thirty-nine, and in what will be the final season of a superb seventeen-year career. He is a full-time designated hitter now, and having a difficult time adjusting to being a hitter and nothing else. His frustration reaches a breaking point during a weekend in Boston. Joe makes his lineup and puts Jorge in the nine hole. An hour before the game, Jorge, in a fit of anger, takes himself out of the lineup. Things only get worse when Brian Cashman goes on national television and details the reason for the late scratch.

Jorge and I have a long talk that night. His emotions run hot, but Jorge is a man who can be honest with himself and make amends if he needs to.

I tell him, "I know you feel disrespected, but this is not you—a guy who refuses to play. Sure, it hurts, but you need to do right by the team, because we need you and we need your bat."

"You're right," he says. "It was just the last straw, but you're right."

Jorge apologizes to Joe and Cashman and gets back to playing ball, and shows what he is about on the most memorable day of the season, standing at home plate in the third inning of a game at Yankee Stadium against the Rays. It is July 9, and Derek has just belted a home run off David Price for his 3,000th big league hit, another staggering achievement in a career chock-full of them. Jorge is the first to greet Derek, and he wraps him up in a massive bear hug, and I am next. Derek is on his way to a 5-for-5 day—a double, a homer, and three singles—as we win, 5–4. Even for someone who doesn't care about milestones, I am filled with joy at this whole experience, seeing a guy Jorge and I have played with for almost twenty years get to a plateau that even players such as Babe Ruth, Joe DiMaggio, and Mickey Mantle never reached.

Jorge is there again two months later, giving the hug to me, on the day I pass Trevor Hoffman and become baseball's all-time saves leader with my 602nd career save. Martin is behind the plate, when I catch the Twins' Chris Parmelee looking at a cutter for strike three and the third out. Jorge is out of the dugout, celebrating before "New York, New York" starts playing. He and Derek push me out to the mound to soak up the applause.

Not long after, Derek and I have a chance to clap for Jorge, when he knocks in the go-ahead run in the victory that clinches another AL East title. Unfortunately, we don't come close to defending our World Series championship. We outhit and outpitch the Tigers in the division series but fall in the decisive Game 5 at

Yankee Stadium. We get ten hits, but very few of them when we need them—the story of the series.

But the other story is our leading hitter, who hits .429 and reaches base in ten of eighteen at-bats. His name is Jorge Posada, and I am proud that he is my catcher, my teammate, and my friend.

Wounded Knee

The outfield has always been my favorite playpen. It's a place where you can roam free, chasing fly balls, trying to outrun them before they hit the ground, defeating gravity. It's where I learned to love the game. There isn't a better feeling in baseball than catching a fly ball on the run.

Even when the Yankees signed me as a pitcher, I still thought of myself as a center fielder.

The next best thing to being an outfielder is playing there in batting practice. Shagging flies, as it is called in baseball slang. A lot of pitchers shag—it's more of a social event than an athletic one. They hang out and talk, and if a fly ball happens to be in the neighborhood, they grab it. That's not how it is for me. I am out there to catch every fly ball I can. I am out there to run hard. Loops around the warning track, running sprints from foul line to foul line, don't do it for me. I want to run and sweat and get dirty. If batting practice is canceled because of rain or because it's a day game after a night game, I am the most bummed-out guy in the ballpark.

A month into the 2012 season, we head to Kansas City for a series with the Royals. We arrive late, so I sleep in and spend the day around the hotel, watching a little Animal Planet before going out to lunch. I get to the park about four o'clock. I haven't pitched since Monday, when I saved a game for Hiroki Kuroda. I don't like to go so long without pitching; I'm hoping to get in the game tonight.

It is a beautiful spring night. I haven't made any official announcement, but I am almost certain this will be my last season, and that makes me want to savor everything, even every pregame fly ball.

I am standing in center field of Kauffman Stadium, wearing a navy blue Yankee jacket and gray running shoes—my shagging uniform. It's almost always windy in Kansas City, and today is no exception. Not far away is our bullpen coach, Mike Harkey, and David Robertson, my bullpen buddy.

Hark is a good soul, a guy who helped launch my career, a fact I remind him of often. The day I won my first major league game in Oakland, the losing pitcher was Mike Harkey, a former No. 1 draft choice of the Chicago Cubs. My teammates that day raked Hark for seven hits and four runs. I was the beneficiary.

"Thanks for throwing all those cookies, Hark," I tell him.

"Happy to help," he replies.

Hark believes in keeping things loose, because by the time the bullpen phone rings late in the game, it's often not relaxed at all. He once said that what he would miss most about me was the element of calm I brought to the pen. I do bring calm, but I also bring mischief. It's amazing how a bunch of grown men turn into a pack of adolescents when you throw them into a bullpen. When I arrive, I fist-bump everybody and then start in, usually with my gum. The command I have with my cutter is nothing compared with what I can do with gum. An earlobe from ten feet away? I nail it almost every time. Either ear. When they are on to my gum heater, I change things up and stick the gum on somebody—Hark, ideally. On the seat of his pants, his back—there are plenty of good spots on Hark's big body. My favorite is his jacket pocket, so when he jams his hand in there it gets good and gooey.

"You got me again," he tells me.

"You're easy," I reply.

Batting practice is almost over when Jayson Nix, just called up from Scranton/Wilkes-Barre, gets into the cage. He hits a long line drive toward the wall in left center and I am off, running hard, eyes fixed on the ball. As I near the warning track, I notice the Kansas City wind is playing tricks again, pushing the ball back toward center. No matter. I am about to make my best catch of the BP session. I feel the crunch of the track beneath my foot as I turn, just slightly, to line up my mitt with the ball.

A shot of pain blasts through my right knee.

It feels as if it's been ripped out of whatever is holding it in place. It's the most pain I have ever felt. The ball bounces onto the track. My momentum takes me into the wall before I crumple to the dirt.

I try to scream, but no sound comes out. My teeth are clenched. Hark and David see my teeth and think I am laughing—goofing around, pretending to be hurt. I am not pretending. My face is in the dirt and my knee is throbbing. I don't know what happened, but

I know it's not good. You know I pray all the time. At home, behind the wheel of the car, on the mound. I am not praying now. The pain is too fierce. I keep rubbing my knee, hoping to take the edge off the pain.

Now Hark, David, and Rafael Soriano, who is also shagging flies, realize that this is real. Hark whistles to Joe Girardi and waves for him to come out.

Joe runs out and so does our assistant trainer, Mark Littlefield. Batting practice stops. I keep writhing.

"Did you hear a pop?" somebody asks.

I shake my head.

"No sound at all?"

"No."

"That's a good sign."

I appreciate the encouraging diagnosis, but it's not an easy sell right now. After a few minutes I am able to sit up. Hark, Joe, and Rafael lift me into the back of a groundskeeper's cart. It has landscaping tools in it, and, now, baseball's all-time saves leader.

"I hope it's okay, Mo," says a fan in the center-field seats.

I wave to the guy as the cart pulls away. A few other fans yell encouraging things, shout my name. I wave again. The whole thing is completely surreal.

What on earth am I doing in the back of this cart? How could something I've done thousands of times result in this?

As the cart continues into the tunnel, I think, *Maybe it's just a sprain, something I can come back from in a week or two.* I get into a waiting car with Mark Littlefield, bound for Kansas University MedWest Hospital for tests. Various scenarios run through my head. I stay positive, because that is my default position, but I also am realistic. I am forty-two years old, and if the news is not good, what happens next?

Could my career actually end face-first on the Kauffman Stadium warning track? One of the sportswriters asks Joe what it would mean if I need knee surgery.

"If that's the report, that's as bad as it gets," Joe says.

We pull up to a boxy brick building where I undergo magnetic resonance imaging on my knee, a half-hour-long procedure that feels like mild jackhammering. The tug of war in my head between optimism and realism keeps raging. When the MRI is finished, I ask the doctor how it looks.

He seems uncomfortable. "I haven't seen the results yet. We're going to get them as soon as we can," he says.

Something tells me he just doesn't want to be the one to deliver bad news. I walk out to the car unaided, putting a good amount of weight on my knee.

It's hard to believe it can really be that bad if I can stand and walk like this, I think.

It's the fifth inning before I am back in the clubhouse. I am not going out to the pen. Somebody else will have to play tricks on Mike Harkey.

I meet with Dr. Vincent Key, the Royals'

team physician. He is a young guy with a goatee and a shaved head like mine.

"I'm sorry to be the one to tell you this, Mariano, but the MRI shows that you have a torn ACL and a torn MCL in your knee," Dr. Key says. "It's going to require surgery. This can have excellent results, but you will almost certainly be out for the rest of the year."

I let his words sink in for a moment:

Torn ACL.

Torn MCL.

Surgery.

Out for the year.

They are hard to take in. Three hours earlier, I am romping around the outfield, doing what I love most, maybe in the last season I'll ever play, savoring every moment. Now I am looking at major reconstructive knee surgery and a long, grinding rehab.

I thank Dr. Key and wait in the clubhouse for the game to end. We lose, 4–3. I stand in front of the whole team. I am fighting tears and not winning. I share my diagnosis with them: Shredded knee. Major surgery. Good-bye, 2012.

Derek gives me a hug. So does Andy. Lots of other guys do, too. This is why I love being on a team. You share your triumphs and your troubles. You are all in it together.

When I meet with the sportswriters, one of the first questions they ask is whether I will definitely come back. I've been dropping hints about retirement since spring training—so they want to know:

Is this how it ends?

Almost instantly, I can feel all sorts of emotions welling up in me. I don't know what to say, or think, and that's pretty much what I tell them: "I don't know."

I do not agonize over things. I cannot undo my knee injury, any more than I can undo the ninth inning of the seventh game of the 2001

World Series. The next morning, my knee is as stiff as a block of cement. Forget about walking unaided. I call Mark Littlefield and ask for crutches. It is not a defeat to have to ask for them. It is the first step to recovery. I am at my locker in the visitors' clubhouse, reporters all around me, not yet twenty-four hours since I lay writhing in the warning-track dirt. I won't be shagging, or saving games, any time soon, but I am not going anywhere.

"I'm coming back. Write it down in big letters. I can't go out this way," I tell the reporters. "Miracles happen; I'm a positive man."

My surgery goes well. I spend the rest of the summer in rehab, treating it as seriously as a World Series appearance. Four or five times a week, three hours a day, I perform an array of torturous exercises to increase my range of motion and strength, pushing, pulling, punishing myself. The pain on many days is as bad as, or worse than, the original injury.

But this is what I need to do if I want to make it all the way back.

If there's one unforeseen positive it is that I discover the joys of summer with my family. I haven't been off for an extended time during a summer since I was twenty years old.

We have a family barbecue on the Fourth of July while the Yankees are winning in Tampa.

I could get used to this, I think.

I go to my boys' ball games, and I am much more in sync with the daily rhythms of our family. Of course, I'm not ready for retirement; I have a comeback season, 2013, ahead of me, Lord willing. But these feelings let me know that when the time comes to retire, I am going to be fine with it.

After two months of rehab, I am feeling so good I am convinced I can pitch this season.

I meet with Dr. Altchek to give him the glowing report.

"Doc, my knee feels great," I say. "I really think that I can—"

He cuts me off. He knows athletes, knows where this is going—that I am about to make a case for why I should get back to the mound this season. He tells me it would be foolish and risky to try to rush back. I am a runner barreling toward home, and he is a Molina brother blocking the plate.

I am not going to get close to scoring.

"Your arm may feel fine, but isn't being a major league pitcher more than that?" he asks. "Can you field bunts? Can you sprint off the mound, plant, turn, and throw a guy out? Can you beat a runner to first on a three-one play?"

I wish I had a counterargument, but he is right.

"I know how much you want to get back to the club for the playoffs, but you're not ready to be on a big league mound yet," Dr. Altchek says. "You should be in great shape for spring training."

As it turns out, they don't need me in the playoffs. We have another disappointing October, beating the Orioles in the division series before getting swept in the ALCS by the Tigers. A bunch of cold bats do us in.

All I can think is: *Hurry, spring.*

NOTES FROM MO

Why I Pray

I may not have been praying while I was writhing in pain on Kauffman Stadium's warning track, but I said plenty of prayers afterward, because prayer is an everyday part of life, as essential to my well-being as eating or sleeping.

I very rarely pray for specific outcomes, though. It's not as if I say to the Lord, "Let us win this World Series game," or "Please let this MRI show no damage." When my agent is negotiating a contract for me, I never get down on my hands and knees and ask the Lord to make me wealthy. Prayer is not a vending machine, where you put in your quarters (or words) and then pull a lever to release the product you want.

For me, the most meaningful prayers are when I ask for God's wisdom. The Lord may not be on the side of the Yankees, but he is on my side. He is always there, ordering my steps if only I will let him. So mostly what I pray for is to hear Him, and to trust in Him. If I do, I know there is nothing to fear, no result that isn't part of the plan. That belief is what allows me to live, and to pitch, in the moment.

Exit Sandman

I am on a back field at our training complex in Tampa, having just spent an hour working on bunt defense and pickoff moves. Mike Harkey, our bullpen coach, is nearby.

"This is it, Hark, I'm done. I'm not going through another year of this."

"You're full of it," Hark says.

"No, this time I mean it," I say.

"You're like the boy who cried wolf," Hark says. "You'll be back here next year and probably the year after and we'll be having the same conversation. You'll never retire."

Hark and I have this exchange often, because spring training is my least favorite time of the year. You hear people say spring training is a new beginning that comes packed with hope. I never really get it. I think I am a homebody at heart. Leaving Clara and the boys has never been easy. I see my sons having fun in the family room right before it is time to leave one year, and I begin to cry.

"I feel like I've failed these boys because I leave them so often," I tell Clara.

Leaving home wasn't easy when I was twenty and it is harder still when I am forty-three. I find comfort in routine, and it's unsettling when the routine gets upended.

It's not that I don't want to prepare and do the work. I understand that there is rust to scrape off, fundamentals to practice, but how many times can you work on your pick-off move? To me, spring training is more boring than waiting for fish to bite. Give me a handful of innings, a couple of weeks, and I'm ready to go. There are so many monotonous drills without the upside: the rush of competition.

In my twenty-fourth and final spring training, though, my attitude is completely different. It's not because I know this will be the last one. It's because I am able-bodied. Nine months after my injury in Kansas City, my knee feels strong. My whole body feels strong. To be running in the outfield and taking ground balls and practicing with the guys— I am so grateful for the opportunity to play again.

I throw a couple of bullpen sessions and make my spring debut on March 9, a few hours after I officially announce my retirement at a press conference. Our opponent is the Atlanta Braves. I get Dan Uggla to pop up for the first out, then strike out Juan Francisco and Chris Johnson to wrap up a quick inning. As first outings go, it couldn't have been better. I am overflowing with optimism.

The good feeling continues into the season. In mid-May I have thirteen saves in thirteen chances, when I return to Kansas City, this time to stand on the mound rather than lie on the warning track. I am not a patient this time around. I am a closer. I like this much better.

It is a day of deep emotion for me, in all kinds of ways. Five hours before the game, I meet with people from the Kansas City community. All season long, at every stop, I make it a point to interact with fans and the ballpark workers who make our games happen, folks who I might not ordinarily get to connect with. In Cleveland, I even get an audience with the legendary drummer John Adams, who has been banging on his drums in the bleachers to incite rallies, almost since the time I was born. I'm not trying to be noble or heroic; I'm simply taking an opportunity to thank people for their contributions. Or, in the case of visiting with people who are facing adversity or tragedy, offering whatever I can to make a difficult time a little better.

The memories of these encounters will stay with me forever, especially the people I met in Kansas City: the Bresette family, who lost their ten-year-old son, Luke, in a freak accident; Jonas Borchert, a fifteen-year-old pitcher who is fighting cancer with all he has; Ricky Hernandez, a young man in a wheelchair who built a playground in his backyard for children with disabilities.

Everybody wants to make a big deal out of how nice it is for me to take an hour out of my day, but it is I who should be thanking them. My life is so much richer for having met these people, and making a bond with them. When I hug Luke's father, Ryan Bresette, I can only express my sorrow and tell him I will pray for his family.

"You are giving us a special gift in a time of a lot of tears," Ryan says.

"You are giving me a gift, too, by sharing

your family and your time with me," I say through tears of my own.

We all have a laugh when another Bresette son, thirteen-year-old Joe, lets it be known that Luke loved baseball but hated the Yankees.

Returning to the scene of the accident isn't traumatic at all. It is a joy. I shag before the game (though I admit I don't go at it as hard as I did before), and I laugh when I see the big "No 'Mo' Zone" sign my teammates have hung on the outfield wall, at the spot where I collapsed. I can't wait to get out there and pitch. In the bullpen, the phone rings in the eighth inning. Hark picks up.

"Mo, you got the ninth," he says.

I come in to save a victory for Andy, who outdueled the Royals' ace, James Shields. I get two outs on grounders to short. Salvador Pérez, the Royals' catcher, hits a double to right and now the hitter is Mike Moustakas, the third baseman. He fouls off four pitches. With the count full, I throw a cutter up and away and he hits it to deep left center, right toward the spot where I got hurt. I turn and watch left fielder Vernon Wells run into the gap and haul it in. It's our fourth straight victory, and we make it five a day later when I save a victory for Kuroda, getting Moustakas again, this time on a short fly to right.

I save twenty-nine games in my first thirty chances and am feeling as good as I ever have. We're up and down as a team, and the barrage of injuries—suffered not just by Derek, who snapped his ankle during the playoffs and hasn't yet fully recovered, but by Mark Teixeira, Curtis Granderson, Francisco Cervelli, and Alex Rodriguez (still recovering from hip surgery)—is like nothing I've ever seen.

We head out west, and at our stop in Oakland I get to visit an old friend, my favorite language teacher, Tim Cooper.

It's been twenty years since we were teammates, but Coop is somebody I won't ever forget. He was there when I needed him, teaching me English and helping me escape my loneliness. I leave him tickets and have him and his family in the dugout before the game. It is great to see him.

"You look good," I tell him.

"I'd cut your hair, but you don't have any," he tells me.

We're six games back as I head for my final All-Star Game, another game I can drive to, since it's at Citi Field, the new home of the New York Mets.

Jim Leyland, the American League manager, calls for me in the bottom of the eighth. When I run through the outfield, "Enter Sandman" starts to play and the fans are standing and cheering. It's not until I am almost at the mound that I realize something.

I am all alone on the field.

Completely alone.

My American League teammates stay back in the dugout to salute me. They are all at the railing, clapping. The National League players are doing the same thing on the first-base side of the field. I am so humbled, so blown away, by the outpouring that I am barely conscious of what I am doing. I bow my head and blow a kiss. I wave my hat and touch my heart, and all I can think is:

How blessed can one man be?

I wish I could go all around Citi Field and thank every single person there.

Before the game, I had told a room full of All-Stars how proud they should be of their accomplishments, and what an honor and privilege it was to be among them. Torii Hunter got up and implored the AL stars to win it for me, getting a rousing cheer as he did a rap-star impersonation.

And now here I am, three hours later, trying to help win it for them, for us. I throw my warm-up pitches to Salvador Pérez with a three-run lead to protect. I retire Jean Segura, Allen Craig, and Carlos Gómez in order. After Gómez grounds to short, I walk slowly toward the third-base dugout. The fans are standing again. This whole season is full of lasts…a last visit to this park, and that stadium, to all these places. It is winding down now. This is my last All-Star team. It's the best imaginable way to go out.

After the break, we are in Chicago for a three-game series against the reeling White Sox. We are not setting the world on fire, either, stuck in fourth in the American League East. But the story of the night isn't our sluggish and inconsistent play or the White Sox's ten-game losing streak. It is the return of Alex Rodriguez, who is finally making his season debut following hip surgery. The hip is the least of Alex's problems, though. He has just been suspended for 211 games for allegedly taking performance-enhancing drugs and then, according to Major League Baseball, trying to block their investigation.

It's the heaviest drug suspension ever handed out and Alex appeals the suspension the same day he gets hit with it, making him eligible to play—and turning the clubhouse in Chicago into a full-blown nuthouse. I've seen World Series games where there wasn't so much commotion, or so many reporters. I don't care. I am happy to have him back. He is no longer in his prime, but he is still a good player who can maybe help get us out of our funk. He is also my friend and my teammate. There are things he has done that I wish he had done differently, but you don't cast aside a teammate because he has made a mistake, or even many mistakes.

When I see Alex at his locker, I go over and give him a hug.

Unfortunately, Alex's return to the lineup doesn't make much of a difference. We get pounded in the opener when Andy has one of the worst starts of his career, and we lose the second game, too. We're now just two games over .500 and have dropped two straight to a club that was out of the pennant race before Memorial Day, which makes the final game of the series that much more important. We need to get righted, and fast, because we're ten and a half games out of first.

CC Sabathia delivers a big effort and we go up, 4–0, early, before the White Sox narrow it to 4–3. I get the ball for the ninth. The fans at U.S. Cellular Field give me a standing ovation on my final visit. I appreciate the sentiment and tip my hat, but I am pretty good by now at getting right down to business. I say my prayer behind the mound. The White Sox's two most dangerous hitters, Alex Ríos and Paul Konerko, are the first two guys I have to face. I get Ríos on a pop-up. Konerko steps in, and on a 0–1 pitch he lifts a short fly to center. Two outs on five pitches, all of them strikes. I like it.

One more and we're out of here, I think.

Gordon Beckham, the second baseman, is at the plate. He has never gotten a hit off of me. I fall behind, 2–1, and leave the next pitch too far out over the plate. Beckham gets good wood on it and drives a double to right center. Now the tying run is at second.

I have thirty-five saves for the year and have blown only two. Adam Dunn is the pinch hitter. I have faced him four times and struck him out four times. I throw two cutters, down and away, and he takes them both for strikes. Doesn't even budge. From the start of my big league career, John Wetteland, the Yankee closer before me, always stressed one thing above all else: Never let yourself get beat with your second-best pitch. When you absolutely need an out, you bring your best. Nothing else.

I need an out. Dunn, a big left-handed power hitter, is going to get another cutter. Dunn's reaction to the first two pitches tells me he is looking inside, so I figure I will stay outside. Austin Romine, the catcher, sets up but my pitch gets too much of the plate. Dunn hits the ball sharply on the ground toward third. I wheel around, just in time to see the ball skip past Alex. Beckham comes around to score. Tie the game.

I am incensed at myself for staying outside with the cutter again. He was so obviously waiting for an inside pitch he'd probably have jumped at it. But I stayed outside, missed my spot, and the game is now tied.

I strike out Carlos Wells to end the inning, but the save is blown. I make the walk that every closer hates: back to the dugout after you've lost the lead, if not the game. It's the longest walk in baseball.

I can't dwell on the failure, though. I have another inning to pitch, and I set them down in order. When Robby crushes a homer in the top of the eleventh, I feel much better. But when the White Sox score two in the bottom of the eleventh, I feel much worse.

We head home to face the Tigers, and it's another supercharged night in The Rodriguez Chronicles—Alex's first game back in the Bronx since his return and since all the uproar about his suspension and appeal. Thousands of people boo him. Thousands cheer him, too. I wonder how the whole thing is going to play out, and if he can stay focused throughout the saga. We take a 3–1 lead into the ninth, and it's my time again.

After I get the first out, Austin Jackson hits a double to left center. I get Torii Hunter on a comebacker. Now Miguel Cabrera, hulking Venezuelan ball crusher, the best hitter in baseball, walks to the plate. Cabrera is hitting .358 with thirty-three home runs (it's early August, mind you). I approach him the same as every other hitter; it doesn't change because of who he is. Sometimes I might pitch to a particular weakness a guy has, but Cabrera doesn't have any weaknesses, so I just go after him.

The Stadium crowd is on its feet. My first pitch is a cutter up in the zone, out over the plate, and Cabrera lofts a fly ball toward the first-base dugout. Lyle Overbay, our first baseman, goes to the railing of the camera well, stretching for the ball, but it falls an inch from his glove. Cabrera gets a big break and he knows it. I get another foul ball to go up, 0–2.

One strike away again.

One strike.

Finish the job. Close this thing, I tell myself.

I throw a ball high out of the zone, but he won't chase. The next pitch is in and Cabrera fights it off, grazing a foul ball off his knee. He hobbles out of the box and the trainer comes out to take a look. After a few minutes he limps back and goes into his stance. I fire again on the inner half, and this time he fouls it off his shin. Now he is limping even more.

All I want is to get this game over with. I try to get him to go after a pitch that breaks off the outside corner. He doesn't bite. The seventh pitch of the at-bat is coming. The way he is swinging at my cutter tells me he could be vulnerable to a two-seam fastball; it's a hard sinker and if I hit the right spot down and in, I think it will get him. It is my best shot, I believe, because it's a given that he is expecting another cutter. I make my deep forward bend and come set, firing the two-seam fastball, violating the Gospel According to Wetteland, because I believe I can fool Cabrera by throwing what he's not expecting. I might've, too, except that the ball goes over the heart of the plate, and just sits there. Now he rips away and the minute he makes contact I drop my head on the mound. I know where it's going to land.

Somewhere over the center-field fence.

"Wow," I say as Cabrera hobbles around the bases. The "wow" is as much about what just happened as it is about Miguel Cabrera's talent with a bat. He handled two pitches that usually would've ended the game. He extended his at-bat.

And he beat me.

For the second time in two games, one strike away from locking down a victory, I make the long walk to the dugout, mission not accomplished, feeling as if I'd taken a punch to the jaw. I have let the guys down.

We win in ten innings on a clutch single by Brett Gardner, so that softens the blow, but the hurt can't be completely erased by the happy ending.

Somebody is going to pay, I tell myself again, same as I did sixteen years earlier in Cleveland, when Sandy Alomar Jr. hit that homer off me in the division series. Somebody is going to pay. How or when they are specifically going to pay, I can't tell you. It's the voice I give to my determination.

What happened tonight is going to make me smarter, stronger, better. It's not going to shake my faith in myself. It doubles my determination to get the next one.

We get drilled on Saturday, so if we want to start turning things around we better get to Justin Verlander on Sunday. Alex hits his first homer of the season into the seats in the second inning, and we lead 4–2 as I take over in the ninth.

The first batter I face is . . . Miguel Cabrera. I bring a sharp cutter that he swings through for 0–1, and after a ball, I put another cutter right on the inside corner. It's 1–2. I go away with a cutter and he takes it for a ball. On 2–2, I am not going the two-seam route, the way I did Friday night.

I am going with Wetteland, and my best. The pitch is up a bit, and it is over the plate. It is not where I wanted it—not at all. I know it before Cabrera even swings. He knocks it over the fence in right and now it is 4–3, and I am on the mound, talking to myself.

How could this happen again? I know he's a great hitter, but I felt in charge of that whole at-bat.

And then, boom—he takes me over the wall again.

I get Prince Fielder on a line drive to third base, and now Víctor Martínez steps in. At 0–1, I come in with a cutter, but again, I miss my spot, and Martínez takes a rip, and there goes another ball into outer space, into the seats in right, tying the game and clinching a history I want no part of: For the first time in my big league career, I've blown three consecutive saves.

I stand on the mound and try to take this in. It is not easy. For the third time in five days, I have failed to do my job. Gardner is the hero again, hitting a game-winning home run off José Veras with two outs in the bottom of the ninth. We take two out of three, no thanks to me. I have seven weeks left in my career. I am not having a crisis in confidence, but I planned on making somebody pay today and nobody did. That really bothers me.

It means everything to me to be dependable, trustworthy.

And I have not been either this week.

A week later, we are in Fenway against the Red Sox, and Sox starter Ryan Dempster decides he's going to drill Alex. After a couple of awkward misses, he finally gets him. I can't believe Dempster is so blatant about it, nor can I believe the way the fans cheer in delight. The venom coming from the stands—what people are screaming at Alex—is ugly. Benches empty. Alex gets his revenge when he homers against Dempster in the sixth, and I wind up with my thirty-sixth save.

But we are five games out of the wild-card spot with five weeks to play. We desperately need to go on a hot streak. Instead we struggle through an up-and-down September, and it becomes clear: My final days as a Yankee are not going to include a pennant race.

Still, it is a very memorable month.

There is Mariano Rivera Day, on September 22, when they retire my number. An amazing day that will last in my memory forever. I pitch a scoreless inning and two-thirds in the game that day. The perfect ending would've been a victory, but we fall, 2–1.

And now, four days later, September 26, 2013, I make the 1,115th and final appearance of my career. It comes against the Tampa Bay Rays. The gate opens in the top of the eighth and I run in from the pen. The crowd stands, chanting my name.

Mah-ree-ah-no.

Mah-ree-ah-no.

I enter with two on and one out, doing my best not to think about the weight of the moment. It is not easy. I retire two batters on six pitches, and then I walk through the dugout and head to the trainer's room in the clubhouse. My forearm is tight. I ask Mark Littlefield to put some hot stuff on it. He is working on my arm when Andy Pettitte walks in.

"What are you doing here?" I ask.

"Jeet and I want to come get you before you finish the ninth. What do you think?" He means they want to get the crowd to give me a standing ovation by taking me out before the game is over, bringing in another reliever so I can have a grand exit.

"Don't do that," I say. "Please don't do it. You guys know me. I want to finish the game. That's my job."

"Okay," Andy says, and off he goes. With my forearm loosened, I go back to the dugout and sit on the bench. I don't move immediately when our at-bat is over. I just sit and look at the mound and the field, before I go out there for the last time.

My last ninth inning in the Bronx.

I have no idea how I am going to get through this. I've held back a flood of emotions so far, but the dam is weakening.

I throw my warm-ups. The crowd stands and cheers again. The first hitter, José Lobatón, slaps a cutter right back to me that takes a high hop. I jump to grab it and make the play.

One out.

The next hitter is Yunel Escobar, the shortstop. He takes a cutter away for 1–0. I come back with another cutter that is up a bit, over the plate, not the best spot by any means, but Escobar swings and lifts a pop-up to Robby Canó.

Two outs.

The next hitter is Ben Zobrist, one of my All-Star teammates at Citi Field. I take a deep breath, hoping I can finish this before the dam breaks, hoping I can do my job one more time.

My last ninth inning as the Yankees' closer.

I need one more out.

I am not going to get it.

Andy and Derek are out of the dugout, walking toward the mound.

I thought I told you not to do this, I think.

They are both wearing mischievous smiles. I cannot help but smile in return.

Andy motions to the home plate umpire that he wants the right-hander from the pen. He and Derek, beloved teammates, both like brothers to me, walk until they reach me. Andy holds out his left hand and I put the ball in it.

I won't be needing it anymore.

My last ninth inning in the Bronx is history. I have thrown my last pitch as a New York Yankee.

Now the dam gives way. I tip my cap to the best fans in baseball and dry my eyes on my sleeve but the finality of it all hits me like a tsunami. Andy wraps his arms around me and lets me collapse into him. I weep like a child in his arms. He holds the back of my head and I allow myself to sob, a fisherman's son who never dreamed he could live a life like this, deep heaves of joy at what I have been given, profound sadness that this part of my journey has come to an end. I am a lucky, lucky man.

The embrace lasts a long time, and then I hug Derek, too, who reassures me. "It's okay," he says. "It's okay."

Matt Daley, the right-hander, arrives from the bullpen—oh yes. There is still a ball game to finish. No closer ever gets used to giving the ball to somebody else.

Is it too late to send him back? I don't really want this to end.

Finally, I am ready. I walk off the mound and wave my hat to the crowd, to my teammates, to the Rays.

When the game ends, I sit in the dugout by myself, just being still, memorizing this place and the power of this moment. The crowd files out. Everybody gives me space.

I decide I need to go back to the mound, my office for the last nineteen years, one more time.

I toe the rubber a couple of times and then bend down and scoop up a handful of dirt and pack it into my right hand. It makes sense to me. I started playing in dirt so I might as well finish playing in dirt.

The perfect keepsake for a simple man.

Glossary

6-4-3 Double Play: For scorekeeping purposes, each position on the baseball field is represented by a number. The pitcher is No. 1, the catcher is 2, the first baseman is 3, and so on. So if the scorekeeper records a "6-4-3" double play it means the shortstop (6) fielded a batted ball, relayed it to the second baseman (4), who stepped on the base (for a force play) or tagged out an advancing runner before throwing to first for the second out. A 6-4-3 or a 4-6-3 double play is the most common "twin-killing" in baseball.

All-Star Game/All-Star Team: Halfway through its 162-game season, Major League Baseball suspends regular play for the All-Star Game. Players are named to the All-Star team by receiving the most votes from fans, except for pitchers, who are named to the team by the managers. (The All-Star team managers are the men whose teams won the previous year's AL and NL championships.) The AL All-Stars play the NL All-Stars in a nine-inning game. Beginning in 2003, the outcome of the game determined which league would have home field advantage for the World Series. The game is always scheduled to take place in mid-July.

Battery: This term refers, collectively, to the pitcher and the catcher.

Bloop/Blooper: Also known as a "Texas Leaguer." A weakly hit ball that drops just over the heads of the infielders but too far for an outfielder to catch for an out.

Convert: What a relief pitcher does when he turns a save opportunity into a win for his team.

Designated Hitter (DH): In the American League, one spot in the lineup is reserved for a player who bats in place of a defensive player (usually the pitcher) and whose only role in the game is to hit. The National League does not usually use designated hitters.

Disabled List (DL): A list of players who are not available to play because of injury. Moving a player to the DL allows a team to bring in another player, usually from the minor leagues, while the injured player is recovering.

Doubleheader: A set of two games played back-to-back on the same day between the same two teams.

Earned Run Average (ERA): A statistic that measures a pitcher's effectiveness by calculating the average number of runs allowed by a pitcher per nine innings. Runs that score because of errors in the field, or passed balls—called "unearned runs"—are not used in calculating ERA.

Fielder's Choice (FC): The action of a defensive player, who fields a batted ball and chooses to get the out on a base runner trying to advance, rather than getting the out on the batter at first base. The batter is not given credit for a hit.

Free Agent: A professional player without a contract, or one whose contract is set to expire at the end of the season, allowing them to negotiate directly with any team, including the one he was playing for at the time his contract expired.

Full Count: A count of three balls and two strikes on a batter. A third strike will result in an out; a fourth ball will grant the batter a walk.

Major League Baseball (MLB): Professional baseball in the U.S. and Canada is governed by Major League Baseball, which oversees the regulation of play in two leagues. The **American League (AL)**, formed in 1901, is composed of fifteen teams in three geographic divisions—East, Central, and West. The **National League (NL)**, founded in 1876, is similarly organized with fifteen teams in the same three geographic divisions.

Minor League Baseball: Also known as the "farm system," or the "bush leagues," the minor leagues are the training grounds for players who hope one day to play in the major leagues. Leagues are organized by player experience and ability.

Rookie Ball is entry-level baseball, for the newest players. The season is just sixty games long.

Single-A is the second-lowest level, but there are subcategories of High-A, for more advanced players, Low-A, and Short-Season A.

Double-A is the second-highest level, and teams in these leagues play in cities, rather than towns, so there is a fan base to support the longer season and bigger stadiums.

Triple-A is the highest level of minor league baseball. Teams at this level play in the biggest U.S. cities without major league teams, such as Columbus, Ohio; Las Vegas, Nevada; and Norfolk, Virginia.

The National Baseball Hall of Fame and Museum: The official museum of baseball, which opened in Cooperstown, New York, in 1939.

No-Hitter: A game in which one team does not get any hits. When a pitcher is throwing a no-hitter, it is traditional for his teammates to not say anything about the no-hitter to the pitcher or anyone else. Some on-air announcers will also avoid specifically mentioning the no-hitter until either an opposing batter gets a hit or the no-hitter is completed.

Perfect Game: A very rare no-hitter in which no batter reaches first base via a hit, a walk, an error or any other means, also referred to in baseball slang as "27 up, 27 down."

Pinch Hitter: A substitute batter who replaces someone (usually the pitcher) in the starting lineup often during a critical situation.

Punch-Out: A strikeout so named because many umpires will make a punch-like signal on the third strike, especially if the batter looks rather than swings at the pitch.

Run Batted In (RBI): An RBI is official credit given to a batter for driving in a run.

Sometimes there is no driving involved—a batter can earn an RBI in a bases-loaded situation by taking a walk, by being hit by a pitch, or by the awarding of first base due to interference. A sacrifice fly or fielder's choice that allows a run to score will also earn the batter an RBI.

Sacrifice Fly: When a batter hits a fly ball to the outfield that is caught for an out, but hit deep enough to allow a runner on base to advance to the next bag, the batter is credited with a sacrifice fly. If a runner scores, the batter is credited with an RBI and is not charged with an at-bat. Also referred to as "sac fly," abbreviated as "SF."

Shutout: A game in which one team prevents its opponent from scoring any runs.

Wild-Card: In Major League Baseball, the wild-card spot in the playoffs is given to the team in each league with the best regular-season record among the second-place teams in each division.

Whiff: A swing at a pitch that completely misses the ball.

Acknowledgments

When you say goodbye to a sport you've played your whole life, as I did in 2013, there's a lot of reflection that goes along with it. When you write your life story in the same year, it makes the reflection, and the soul-searching, that much deeper.

Writing *The Closer,* in many ways, was not unlike getting a save. I may be the one with the statistic (or my name on the cover), but a whole team full of people made huge contributions to allow that to happen. I could fill another chapter with the names of all the people I am deeply grateful to, and I hope and pray that any omissions here are understood to be due to limitations of space and my flawed memory, and not to what I feel in my heart.

Fernando Cuza has been my baseball agent, friend, and right-hand man for many years, and he and Relativity Sports senior vice president Aaron Spiewak were the guiding forces and caretakers of the book from the outset. Aaron, in particular, found the book a home with Little, Brown, a top-notch publishing house with top-notch people who have been with me from the very early innings of this project, starting with publisher Reagan Arthur. Senior production editor Karen Landry and staff did a remarkable job turning a manuscript into a finished book, just as publicists Elizabeth Garriga and Nicole Dewey did in getting the word out, creatively and persistently, about *The Closer*. John Parsley, my editor, is not just skillful at his job; he was a tireless and indispensable ally from start to finish. Thanks, too, to John's able assistant, Malin von Euler-Hogan.

Jason Zillo, the Yankees director of media relations, has been there for me throughout the years, a constant source of support and counsel, never more than in my farewell tour in 2013.

My first catcher and friend of twenty-five years, Claudino Hernandez, along with our Panama Oeste teammate Emilio Gaes, saw the possibilities for me before I did; how do you thank somebody for *that*? Claudino also doubled as a driver / Puerto Caimito tour guide for Wayne Coffey, my coauthor, when he went to Panama to conduct research. Wayne and I began this book with a prayer, asking for the Lord's strength and guidance so that my story would honor Him even as it tells the story of a humble man who has as many shortcomings as any other man. I believe our prayer was answered. In our countless hours together shaping the manuscript, Wayne helped draw out memories and find an honest and authentic way for me to interweave all the elements of my journey. Along the way, I discovered that writing a book is hard work, but also deeply rewarding work.

I would also be remiss if I didn't thank

Wayne's wife, Denise Willi, and their children, Alexandra, Sean, and Samantha, for their patience; they did not see or hear much from my coauthor as we neared the finish line. Frank Coffey and Sean Coffey were among the early readers whose insights were invaluable. Wayne's literary agent, Esther Newberg of ICM, along with her associate, Colin Graham, put together our collaboration with Relativity, which set Wayne and me on our way. The esteemed sports team with whom Wayne works at the *New York Daily News*— Teri Thompson, Bill Price, Eric Barrow, Mike Matvey, and Ian Powers—were likewise staunch supporters, and I thank them for that.

My parents and siblings and cousins—most of them still in and around Puerto Caimito— were the foundation of my life before anybody knew who I was, and in so many ways shaped the man I became. I can't say that fans and players and employees of the clubs around the big leagues had any part in shaping me, but they did so much to make this journey of mine special. To all the people I met and the clubs that honored me in 2013—to the fans of Detroit, Cleveland, Tampa Bay, Colorado, Kansas City, Baltimore, the Mets, Seattle, Oakland, the Angels, Minnesota, Texas, the Dodgers, San Diego, the White Sox, Boston, and Houston—I just hope with all my heart that you know how much your kindness and tributes touched me. To the fans of the New York Yankees: Well, you were there in the beginning and you were there at the end, and I will never forget the love and support you've shown me all these years. I never wanted to be anybody's closer but yours. So I'll just say thank you all, and bless you all.

It's almost impossible for me to describe how important Mario and Naomi Gandia are to the Rivera family—both as loving extended family members and as sources of Christian inspiration and wisdom. As much as any people I know, Mario and Naomi live in the Lord's light, share the Lord's love, and make the world better because of it. They always want to be behind the scenes, but just this once, they must be out front.

There aren't enough words in my native tongue, Spanish, or in English to convey the love and admiration I have for my wife, Clara. She is the rock of our family life, a very present help in good times and otherwise. To our boys, Mariano Jr., Jafet, and Jaziel, you are the greatest gift a father can have, and I am as proud of the young people you are as I am grateful for your love. I have been away for many times in your life, and one of the best things about retirement is that I can stop saying goodbye so often.

And to the Lord, who has blessed me with His grace and mercy, whose wisdom and love are the beacons of my life, I don't want to just say thank you. I want to glorify You and honor You with all I do, and pray that *The Closer* is a good way to start.

About the Authors

MARIANO RIVERA was a New York Yankee for nineteen seasons. He is Major League Baseball's all-time saves and postseason ERA leader, a thirteen-time All-Star, and a five-time world champion. He and his wife, Clara, have three sons and live in New York.

WAYNE COFFEY is one of the country's most acclaimed sports journalists. A writer for the *New York Daily News*, he cowrote R. A. Dickey's bestselling *Wherever I Wind Up* and is the author of the *New York Times* bestseller *The Boys of Winter*, among other books. He lives in the Hudson Valley with his wife and children.

Sue Corbett is the author of several books for children, including *Free Baseball* and *The Last Newspaper Boy in America*. She is also a regular contributor to *Publishers Weekly* and *People* magazine. She lives in Virginia with her family.